GOOK
JOHN MCCAIN'S RACISM
AND WHY IT MATTERS

Gook
John McCain's
RACISM
AND WHY IT MATTERS

Irwin A. Tang

The it Works/Paul Revere Books

Gook: John McCain's Racism and Why It Matters

Copyright © 2008 by Irwin A. Tang

Cover and book design by Maura Murnane.

The it Works / Paul Revere Books is located in Austin, Texas. All questions and requests should be addressed to The it Works Publishing by email at the.it.works. publishing@gmail.com.

Additional copies of this book are available at www.irwinbooks.com.

First edition, first printing, June 2008.

Library of Congress Cataloguing–In Publication Data

Tang, Irwin

Gook: John McCain's Racism and Why It Matters

ISBN 0-967-9433-4-3

Printed in the United States of America

TABLE OF CONTENTS

for my family

Introduction

My mother does not want me to publish this book. She called me this morning. She told me she had thought about it over the weekend, and she had come to a conclusion. *Be nice to John McCain.*

She didn't say, "Be nice to him because he's a war hero." She didn't say, "Because he's a senior senator."

I knew exactly what she meant even though she did not say it.

I grew up in East Texas and my parents still live there. I love my hometown, but the Ku Klux Klan is still very active there. Black people still get "nigger" yelled at them there. Asians still get trash dumped on them by roving bands of racists.

John McCain has a history of endorsing white supremacists and racist activists, putting them on his payroll and simply consorting with them. Perhaps they call themselves "Neo-Confederates." Perhaps they are associated with a right-wing "militia." Perhaps they call themselves "Council of Conservative Citizens" (discussed later).

Whatever the case, white supremacy groups have been, through the course of American history, the most successful terrorists ever to operate in this nation.

Growing up, I feared the KKK more than my parents did, or even my sister.

I was the one who discovered the noose. It was hanging from a branch of the oldest tree in our front yard. I was twelve or thirteen, and I woke up on a Sunday morning and saw the noose from my bedroom window.

I went outside, and I looked through the noose. I could have slipped it around my neck, that's the height it was hanging at. Somehow I knew that the noose was meant for me.

For years, I wondered who had hung the noose. Today I know. I know because I've learned a bit about the habits of the Klan. The KKK took a bat to our mailbox, right after my father spoke up against them. I, too, organized against the KKK when I was in college.

The KKK has a good long history of attacking Asian Americans here in Texas. Ask the Vietnamese Americans on the Texas coast what they went through in the 1970s and 1980s. It was the closest to a race war we have seen in recent American history.

To the KKK, we are just "gooks."

"I hate the gooks," said John McCain in the year 2000. "I will hate them as long as I live."

It doesn't matter who John McCain is calling a "gook." It reveals something when a senator calls people "gooks" and volunteers it for mass media broadcast. If nothing else, it means this senator is very different from the rest of us.

No matter who Mr. McCain is calling "gooks," he is using *racist* language to express what he himself admits is a deep *hatred*.

The fact that Mr. McCain carries such everlasting hate within him — that says something too. Add to this his much-celebrated rage, his history of physically attacking those he disagrees with, and his consistent eagerness to start wars, and you have a very unique senator. *One that I should be nice to.*

And that's what my mom meant.

She does not know the details of McCain's activities in connection with white supremacists. She does not know of the lobbyists on his campaign who have worked for the types of dictators, terrorists, and political parties that my parents escaped from China to avoid. Indeed, some of those foreign governments who have hired McCain's lobbyists have agents working for them in the United States.

My mother does have some idea of the types of "dirty tricksters" John McCain has on his campaign team. Anyone paying attention knows that these people will spare no time in "swiftboating" anyone considered an "enemy" of their camp. The fear that my family or I might be "swiftboated" is an absolutely sincere fear, an absolutely justified fear, as is the fear that the Klan might seek revenge on me and my family.

My mother... my mother simply wants no trouble, no heartache, for me or my family. My parents have suffered enough in their lives. Mr. McCain speaks a great deal of honor. I write this book with the most honorable intentions, and I hope that Mr. McCain and his supporters will respect that.

There are yet other reasons why I should stop working on this book.

Have you ever been an object before? More specifically, have you ever been an object that you cannot identify? It is difficult to describe my own personal experience as a "gook" in America, or, as Bao Nguyen scrawled on his spit-smeared shirt, an "American Gook" (discussed later).

I got spit on for being Asian only once or twice growing up. I was called "gook" every so often. Other times it was "Jap" or "Chink" or some other racial epithet. I was blamed for every conceivable U.S. war. Despite my being Chinese American and far too young, people harassed *me* for bombing Pearl Harbor. Because I was Asian, I was labeled "Commie," "Vietcong," "V.C.," and "Charlie." Revenge had to be exacted upon me.

Not much changed in college, as the university ROTC trotted by and taunted me with some chant about dropping napalm explosives on Vietnamese babies. The anti-racism shanty I helped to construct was desecrated with the words "KKK," "White Power," and other "warnings."

The name-calling was never as bad as the violence. I was a skinny "Oriental" kid, as we were called then. When two or three of my racist tormentors ganged up on me, it was not clear to me that I would survive, or if I did, it would be in any desired condition.

But I got lucky. Usually, when I was called "gook," or when someone would glare at me and say it without saying it, that person only sneered and spit on the ground as if I had done something to his momma. And most of the time I was physically attacked, I managed to keep myself relatively uninjured.

What I should have learned from my first twenty-two years, all spent in East Texas, was this: when someone calls you a "gook," just walk away. Wipe the figurative spit off of your face and move on.

Imagine working on a book hour after hour, and each hour you work on that book, you're reminded that in some ways, to some people, you are some sort of object, and you can't really say what kind of object. You just know that you are not really there, and yet you are. But this cannot stop me from writing. In fact, it propels me, as I attempt to better understand what it means to be this object.

One reason to stop writing speaks softly to me, convincingly. My mother told me essentially not to write a negative book. Write a positive one.

My mother is a Christian, and although I have never converted to Christianity, I learn every day to more deeply appreciate the philosophy of Jesus Christ.

A childhood friend explained a facet of Jesus's way to me. He said that Christ believed not in fighting evil but in helping those in need.

Millions of people each year die because our world is so much more interested in fighting "evil" than helping those in need. Many of those people are innocent civilians killed in some war against people who are really, truly evil. But those evil people live in the house of the innocent civilians, and when one is bombed, all are killed.

I am one of that silent majority that believes that if we spent the war budget on feeding the hungry, sheltering the homeless, and treating the sick, there'd be much less need for any war.

But some people in this world need wars. And some people in this world need "gooks." Many times, those are the same people. And that is what this book is largely about: *the terrible overlap of racism and war.*

Dear Mother, I am not "warring" against anyone. I don't mean to hurt John McCain or the Republican Party. I don't want them to stress or feel pain or get angry or depressed.

All I wish is for the American people — *my people* — to question themselves and question Mr. McCain. To make an informed, careful decision at this, the world's crossroads.

What I am doing here is not an attack. It is a public service for my nation. This book is a public service for our beloved kaleidoscopic polyglot of peoples, cultures, and individuals known as America. And yes, this book is for all those people, like my parents, and like John McCain, who have survived war.

My paternal grandfather was a soldier, much like John McCain's grandfather, Slew McCain. My grandfather served in the Chinese Nationalist Army. He fought the Japanese in World War II and fought the Chinese Communists on more than one occasion. He spent half of his life with a gun in his hand.

My father, my mother, and my uncles and aunts were all civilian refugees of those wars. As a result of war, my father lost three siblings and my mother lost one sibling. My parents' generation was "collateral damage" — civilian casualties. Although my parents survived, they are not unscarred.

I wish to help prevent the next unnecessary war, the next unnecessary arming of terrorists and dictators.

As I write, millions of people in Myanmar and China are homeless, hungry, and diseased as a result of a furious cyclone and a powerful earthquake. As I write, American emergency relief for such disasters is measured by the millions of dollars, while the amount allocated for war is measured by the hundreds of *billions*.

Hundreds of thousands of Iraqis lay in the ground because of an invasion and the resulting civil war. There are several parties in Iraq, all believing that they are fighting evil. Of course, we Americans believe that one party is sincere and true.

Whoever is right or whoever is wrong, a bullet is a bullet. And hundreds of thousands have died violently; millions live in fear.

We Americans never really contemplated this possibility. Most of us spent the better part of half an hour wondering what might happen to the civilians in a war in Iraq. What might happen if we are not accepted as liberators? What might happen if factions do not unite immediately?

Why is it that we did not ask these questions before we started launching missiles? Why is it that our highest leaders seemed so sure that everything would go right? Why were they so sure that putting the lives of millions of people at risk by executing their plan was the right thing to do?

For those who think in terms of "gooks" or any other racial epithet ("nigger"), war is not so difficult a question. Make war or help the needy? Make war. Even the civilians are "gooks."

To the Japanese invaders, my parents were "gooks."

The confused might say, "Do you mean that your grandfather should not have fought the Japanese?"

My argument here in this book is not a sweeping condemnation of all violent activities. Of course my grandfather's defense of his nation was right. In fact, the Chinese had no other choice but to wage war against the invading armies.

I argue against the transformation of people into "gooks." Into something subhuman. Foreign, poor people, though, are often never "people" to begin with. Not in the eyes of the powerful. They start, and end, as something not quite people.

John McCain is a hero of the Vietnam War. Despite this fact, his understanding of war and his attitude toward race both seem overly simplistic and quite troubling. The two issues are intimately linked, not only in the mind of John McCain, but in the soul of our nation. If you've ever been called a "gook," you know this in your heart.

INTRODUCTION   7

Chapter 01
Gook: A History

"I hate the gooks. I will hate them as long as I live."

—John McCain, on his presidential campaign bus, February 17, 2000, as reported by the *San Francisco Chronicle.*

"I hated the gooks and will continue to hate them as long as I live."

—John McCain, February 17, 2000, as reported by the *Washington Post.*

"The Haitians, in whose service United States Marines are presumably restoring peace and order in Haiti, are nick-named 'Gooks' and have been treated with every variety of contempt, insult and bestiality."

Herbert J. Seligman, *The Nation,* 1920.

Thus was born a racial epithet. Seligman was the first to document the use of the the word "gook."

The term "gook" was invented to insult and dehumanize black people. They were Haitians to be exact, and they were enduring one of the United States' various military occupations of nations in the Caribbean and Latin America.

The exact origin of "gook" is unknown. It is very likely related to the term "goo goo," a term the U.S. military applied to Filipinos during the U.S. war to conquer the Philippines. That war lasted from 1898 to about 1902 or so, depending on when one decides the mission had been accomplished.

In the early years, it seems, many American soldiers had difficulty categorizing the Filipinos racially. They called them "niggers." Wrote U.S. serviceman Henry Loomis Nelson, "Our troops in the Philippines... look upon all Filipinos as of one race and condition, and being dark men, they are therefore 'niggers,' and entitled to all the contempt and harsh treatment administered by white overlords to the most inferior races." (Kramer, 128) Paul A. Kramer described the evolution of "goo-goo" from "nigger" in his book, *The Blood of Government*. As American soldiers tried to categorize the Filipinos into their own taxonomy of race and culture, they compared Filipinos to African Americans, and some decided that Filipinos were very different from Americans, both black and white. One American soldier stated that "it is nothing to see a niger (we call them nigers) woman pretty near naked."

When Peter Lewis of New York was sent in January 1902 to supervise a thousand Filipino women allowed out of a "reconcentration camp" (concentration camp) to collect "palay," he described the scene as being like "the American niggers picking cotton." It was striking that he felt compelled to modify "nigger" with "American"; it suggests that the Filipinos were "Asian niggers."

One black soldier complained that white soldiers "talked with impunity of 'niggers' to our soldiers, never once thinking that they were talking to home 'niggers.'" When reminded that "at home this is the same vile epithet they hurl at us," these soldiers "beg pardon and make some effeminate [sic] excuse about what the Filipino is called." Perhaps as a way of distinguishing Filipinos from blacks, white soldiers decided to refer to Filipinos as "goo-goos." So within a twenty year span in American imperial history, Filipinos were called "niggers" and Haitans were called "gooks."

Where the term "goo-goo" originated is unknown, exactly, but Kramer offers a very plausible explanation:

> According to Freeman, among the songs sung by U.S. troops on the long voyage from San Francisco had been a minstrel tune with the chorus "Just because she made dem goo-goo eyes." When American soldiers first "gazed into the dark orbs of a Filipino *dalaga* [young woman]" on arrival, they had commented to each other, "Gee, but that girl can make goo-goo eyes.'" Filipino men had taken the term as an insult; when American soldiers learned this, "it stuck, and became a veritable taunt."

Kramer refers to a man named Freeman whose story describes U.S. soldiers reading into the eyes of Filipino girls and women sexual desire and promiscuity. Of course, this was just another way of dehumanizing and degrading Filipinos, and so the "goo-goo" epithet seemed to be a way to make whores of Filipina women and to emasculate Filipino men. According to Kramer, white soldiers spat on Filipinos, pushed them off of sidewalks, and essentially made racist degradation a part of the standard military operation, while black soldiers tended to eschew such acts. Some Filipinos understood the mistreatment of blacks in America and appealed to their black brothers to stop their oppression of the Filipinos and instead fight their battle in America — where blacks were treated like Filipinos. At that time, blacks in America were castrated, lynched, spat upon, and treated as animals.

Filipinos were treated in many ways worse than animals. They were slaughtered by the hundreds of thousands. The terms "goo-goo" and "gook" have been tools in some of American history's bloodiest and most disturbing wars.

The straight-talking American historian Howard Zinn cites a report from the Philadelphia *Ledger*:

> The present war is no bloodless, opera bouffe engagement; our men have been relentless, have killed to exterminate men, women, children, prisoners and captives, active insurgents and suspected people from lads of ten up, the idea prevailing that the Filipino as such was little better than a dog.... Our soldiers have pumped salt water into men to make them talk, and have taken prisoners people who held up their hands and peacefully surrendered, and an hour later, without an atom of evidence to show that they were even insurrectos, stood them on a bridge and shot them down one by one, to drop into the water below and float down, as examples to those who found their bullet-loaded corpses.

Although the United States was invading the Philippines, the Filipino soldiers were characterized as "insurrectos," as if the United States was putting down an insurrection.

One U.S. general returning from the Philippines province of Luzon reported in 1901 that one-sixth of the population of Luzon had been killed by U.S. soldiers or died of dengue fever during the war. In Batanga, it was estimated by the secretary of that province that one-third of the population had died by combat, disease, or famine.

A major portion of Filipinos — likely the vast majority — wanted to remain independent of the United States. President McKinley and then President Theodore Roosevelt, other politicians, and American big business wanted to keep the nation, which the U.S. had recently "taken" from Spain in the Spanish-American War. They were willing to kill as many Filipinos as necessary to expand the American empire. But many Americans understood this, and found it disgusting.

The great American writer William James declared, "God damn the U.S. for its vile conduct in the Philippine Isles."

Mark Twain wrote:

> We have pacified some thousands of islanders and buried
> them; destroyed their fields; burned their villages, and
> turned their widows and orphans out-of-doors; furnished
> heartbreak by exile to some dozens of disagreeable patri-
> ots; subjugated the remaining ten millions by Benevolent
> Assimilation, which is the pious new name of the musket;
> we have acquired property in the three hundred concu-
> bines and other slaves of our business partner, the Sultan
> of Sulu, and hoisted our protecting flag over that swag.
>
> And so, by these Providences of God — and the phrase is
> the government's, not mine — we are a World Power.

Although the U.S. conquest of the Philippines is largely forgotten, the war
established new precedents by its treatment of the Filipinos.

> 1) "Scorched earth" policy. The mass slaughter of civil-
> ians through bombing, shooting, disease, famine, arson,
> homelessness, and war-induced famine was established
> as an effective means of advancing military and political
> goals. In this "scorched earth" policy, civilians were killed,
> their villages burned down, and survivors turned home-
> less. Some say the U.S. employed this method in Vietnam.
>
> 2) The military learned that terms such as "nigger" or
> "goo-goo" were useful in dehumanizing local popula-
> tions and united U.S. soldiers against a common "them."
> The psychological warfare, in practice if not in purpose,
> demeaned the population while making it easier for U.S.
> soldiers to commit war crimes against civilians.
>
> 3) The systematic use of torture against innocent civil-
> ians as both a form of information gathering and a form of
> terrorism. The most common torture was the "water tor-

ture." U.S. military men opened Filipinos' mouths up with bayonets. They pumped water into their stomachs until the man, woman, or child's stomach was filled to bursting. Some persons' stomachs did burst. After a person's stomach was prepared, a heavy American soldier would jump on the person's stomach, sending the water shooting out of the mouth, or simply exploding that person's organs.

4) The use of concentration camps (or "reconcentration camps") to stuff Filipino women, men, and children into until they die of the horrendous conditions there or until the U.S. was prepared to release them.

Even after Theodore Roosevelt declared victory in the Philippines, the massacres continued, and so did the racial degradation. In an article for the Philippines History Group of Los Angeles entitled, "The Balangiga Massacre: Getting Even," Victor Nebrida writes:

In the diaries of other [American] soldiers are descriptions of the destruction of rice crops and the slaughter of domestic animals followed by homely accounts of kindness received from fellow troopers and surprise reunions with former neighbors from back home. Claude F. Line, a young private, described not only his love of home and family, but also his delight at terrifying two Filipino civilians. "They were the first goo–goos I ever saw turn white." (http://www.bibingka.com/phg/balangiga/default.htm)

The fact that the Filipinos were "goo–goos" allowed the American soldiers to kill, torture, and do what they wished to them without any regard to the morals and religion they left at home. Dr. Richard E. Welch, a historian at Lafayette College, provides evidence of how racism allows for more easily committed war crimes:

In many letters there is an eerie contrast between the writers' disregard for the slaughter of Filipino goo–goos and their concern for the health of their parents and friends. William Eggenberger described with boyish glee an incident in which he and a fellow private had terrorized the inhabitants of a nipa hut by sticking their bayonets through the side of the house. He then concluded his letter with the request: "Don't you and the old man work so hard all the time... hoping these lines will find you all in the best of health, a kiss for you all." ("American Atrocities in the Philippines: The Indictment and the Response," by Richard E. Welch, Jr., *The Pacific Historical Review*, Vol. 43, No. 2 (May, 1974), pp. 233–253)

George Frisbie Hoar, Republican Senator from Massachusetts, spoke to the U.S. Senate on May 22, 1902, as the American conquest of the Philippines raged on:

> You have devastated provinces. You have slain uncounted thousands of peoples you desire to benefit. You have established reconcentration camps... You make the American flag in the eyes of a numerous people the emblem of sacrilege in Christian churches, and of the burning of human dwellings, and of the horror of the water torture.

Hoar was a true Republican Party maverick. With his three–hour speech, he risked offending the fiery Republican president, Theodore Roosevelt (McCain's hero), who relished the bloody conquest of the Filipinos.

Torture, mass killings, and even slavery followed the racial epithet "goo–goo" as it transformed into "gook" and was applied against Haitians. On July 10, 1920, Herbert J. Seligman reported from Haiti:

> The five years of American [military] occupation, from 1915 to 1920, have served as a commentary upon the white civilization which still burns black men and women at the stake. For Haitian men, women, and children, to a number estimated at 3,000, innocent for the most part of any offense, have been shot down by American machine gun

and rifle bullets; black men and women have been put to torture to make them give information; theft, arson, and murder have been committed almost with impunity upon the persons and property of Haitians by white men wearing the uniform of the United States. Black men have been driven to retreat to the hills from actual slavery imposed upon them by white Americans, and to resist the armed invader with fantastic arsenals of ancient horse pistols, Spanish cutlasses, Napoleonic sabres, French carbines, and even flintlocks. In this five years' massacre of Haitians less than twenty Americans have been killed or wounded in action.

Of all this Americans at home have been kept in the profoundest ignorance. The correspondent of the Associated Press in Cape Haitien informed me in April, 1920, that he had found it impossible in the preceding three years, owing to military censorship, to send a single cable dispatch concerning military operations in Haiti, to the United States. Newspapers have been suppressed in Port au Prince and their editors placed in jail on purely political grounds. Even United States citizens in Haiti told me of their fear that if they too frankly criticized "the Occupation," existence in Haiti would be made unpleasant for them. [published in *The Nation*]

The word "gook" was firmly established, then, not far off the coast of Florida, as a term used against people of color. As the word gained usage during various U.S. military actions, it seemed to take on the meaning, "subhuman nonwhite people."

Jules Archer explained that the U.S. Marines in Haiti

talked as casually of shooting "gooks" as sportsmen talked of duck–hunting. Patrolling against the Cacos, some Marine officers looted the homes of native families they were supposed to protect. Others talked of 'cleaning out' the island by killing the entire native population. Prisoners were beaten and tortured to make them tell what they knew about Cacos' whereabouts. Some were allowed to "escape," then were shot as they fled.

According to one scholar, "gook" had been in use as early as 1893 to refer in a demeaning fashion to a promiscuous woman. Thus, the racial epithet took on its own sexist meaning. Perhaps U.S. soldiers called the prostitutes that they patronized "gooks," and then began using the word to describe all local people.

The word "gook" was likely applied against numerous Latin American peoples as the United States, from 1850 to 1992, orchestrated dozens of military invasions, insurrections, and coups in Latin America. "Gook" was certainly applied to the people of Nicaragua during the Marines' invasion of that nation in 1926; perhaps "gook" became popular there because the Nicaraguan mission was one of the more challenging ones of that time.

> There is a Marine Patrol arranged by the new president to find Sandino. There will be a bunch of "gook generals" to lead the disguised Marines to all of the bandits. The Marines are accompanying the Moncade Volunter National Troops, of whom are mostly ex-bandits. (from the letters of Emil (Porter) Thomas, 1923 to 1929, available from Ohio University, *https://www.library.ohiou.edu/archives/mss/mss192.pdf*)

The Marines were after the rebel leader Sandino. Apparently, the soldiers referred to both enemy and friendly Nicaraguans as "gooks." Perhaps the best article ever written about the word "gook" was published in 1999. Dave Roediger describes the evolution of "gook" into the mid–twentieth century:

> By the time of the Second World War, the identity of the gook expanded again. The West Coast's brilliant amateur student of language, Peter Tamony, took notes on radio commentator Deane Dickason's 1943 comments on gook—

the Marines' "word for natives everywhere" but especially for Arabs. The latter of Dickason's conclusions is likely closer to the mark than the former. "Natives" of France, or of Britain, or of Holland, were not gooks, but people of color were. In particular, the mainly Arab population of North Africa acquired the status of gook. Indeed the usage spread to French colonialists so that, even a decade after the war, panicked settlers reacted to Algeria's national liberation struggle by indiscriminately slaughtering villagers in "gook–hunts."

In the Pacific, the Second World War witnessed the spread of gook to apply to peoples far beyond the Philippines. And coming from a nation supporting the United States or from an American territory was not proof against being called a gook. At the war's end, large riots between servicemen and natives erupted in Hawaii. *Life* commented in November 1945 that the rioting servicemen saw their enemies as "gooks—that stupid, dirty lower strata of Honolulu citizen." The San Francisco News explained to a California audience that same month that gook was "a Hawaii servicemen's name roughly equivalent to the mainland "zoot–suiter" — the latter term describing the stylishly dressed Hispanics and blacks who were often the victims of mob violence stateside.

Interestingly, "gook" overlapped again with "nigger," as American soldiers have also called Arabs "sand niggers."

While the word "gook" may have been applied to Chinese during various American occupations of that nation, American soldiers applied the word to large numbers of Asians for the first time during the Korean War. In fact, the Korean War brought the word into its widest use to date. The American military fought both the North Koreans and the Communist Chinese army, so the application of the word "gook" can be said to have been pan–Asian or at least multi-ethnic. Nevertheless, the word seemed much more specific to Koreans. To provide an example of how "gook" was used in Korea, see this comment posted to the Korean War Project website by a Marine Corps veteran of the Korean War:

> One last gem, bunch of gook peasants demanded we vacate our CP, so they could return to their village site; plus, they angrily didn't like their temple turned into our Ammo dump. Capt. Saunders told gooks, to their teeth, to go back to their hobo village up the road– if not – he will march his AT-7 Marines with fixed bayonets and route these ungrateful gook bastards to North Goonyland. Yes, these were just some of the macabre day to day incidents in the asshole of the world – KOREA –. Thank God, the CORPS started R&R to Japan to ease our nerves. (http://www.koreanwar.org/ html/units/usmc/7mareg_at.htm)

The racial slur "gook" was pronounced the same as the word for "people" in Korea. Koreans call themselves "Hangook," meaning "Korean people." In a brilliant, if accidental, stroke of racist perversity, American military personnel turned what Koreans called themselves into an insulting racist tag for all Koreans. "Gook" was not a bastardization of the word "Hangook," but rather an attempted bastardization of the Korean people from their own history and pride. Malcolm X, despite his own racist tendencies, had brilliant observations concerning race relations on this Earth. Speaking of black Americans, X told *Playboy* magazine, "The white man has taught the black people of this country to hate themselves as inferior, to hate each other, to be divided against each other." The word "gook" has taught tens or hundreds of millions of people around the world that they are inferior. By applying "gook" to Koreans, American forces caused the Koreans to dehumanize themselves by calling themselves "Korean" in their own language.

But the most interesting development in Korea was that Americans referred to both the South Koreans and North Koreans as "gooks." The Americans were allied with the South Koreans. Roediger notes that the U.S. military attempted to tamp down on the racist terminology in Korea, as it gave the impression to Asians that the United States was a racist imperialist force. But the efforts did not work. By labeling both Korean "enemies" and "friends" as "gooks," officers and foot soldiers, bureaucrats and common Americans devalued the work of the soldiers. After all, they were fighting against "gooks" for the sake of "gooks." It gave credence to the idea, long-held throughout the Western world, that all Koreans and all Asians were the same. It seemed to indicate that the war had no larger meaning; that the Communists and the supposed Democrats were all the same, that the war was simply a matter of "capitalist" nations and "communist" nations fighting over land masses and the wealth that came with them.

There were psychological benefits to calling both enemy and friend "gook." By dehumanizing all of the local populations — enemy or not — all forms of violence could be more easily reconciled with the sense of right and wrong that soldiers had learned growing up. Empathy was easier to discard, when it was believed that the targeted people were not really people. It was easier to drop bombs on civilians, burn down their villages, apply various tortures, and so forth.

War correspondent Robert Kaiser reported in 1969, "The only good gook, it is said again and again on US bases throughout Vietnam, is a dead gook." On this common axiom of the Vietnam War, Roediger writes, "The stark dehumanization of enemies in such a line reminds us that racism is not only a way to motivate fighters in wars of aggression but also that militarism has helped foster racism."

"Gook" was used even in the most mundane circumstances, such as describing where unusable blood is taken. Here is an exchange between an American hospital lab technician and a reporter, as documented in 1970:

> "We use just about all the blood we get. We're in sort of a slump now — not much action — so we got quite a bit on hand."
>
> "What do you do with it when it gets too old?"

"Give it to the gook hospitals." (James Sterba reporting in
The New York Times Magazine, Oct. 18, 1970)

The most insightful commentary I've seen on the meaning of "gook" was testimony given by Lance-Corporal Kenneth Campbell ("A" Battery, 1st Battalion, 1st Marine Division) during the House of Representatives War Crimes Hearings held on April 29, 1971.

Asked a question about the killing of civilians, Campbell responded to the committee.

> Lance-Corporal Kenneth Campbell: I think the type of warfare and also, you know, the policies that are passed down to the individual troops, you know, Free-Fire Zones, I do not know how many times I fired arty [artillery] in a Free-Fire Zone where everything in there was supposed to be enemy, where I knew myself there were quite a few civilians. These type of things. And also the training we get before we go there and while we are there, all lend to the atrocities. Conventional warfare, the use of arty and air power, I think it is ridiculous to try to use that in a guerrilla war because just from, well, just from, I don't know, luck, whatever you want to call it, bad luck, there is always bound to be a certain percentage of civilians killed by the use of heavy arms such as arty and air power. I mean, how can you kill a guerrilla among a bunch of civilians by dropping bombs?

> Congressman Ron Dellums: I would like to ask in extension of that, are you familiar with the term that the only good gook is a dead gook?

> Campbell: I am very familiar with that.

> Dellums: In your personal opinion and experience, did

that term refer not only to VC but to [South Vietnamese] people as well?

Campbell: That was the general attitude. "The only good gook was a dead gook," and that referred to Vietnamese, to gooks, you know. Like I said, gooks were anybody, anybody with slanted eyes, they were not just VC and NVA. So, therefore, if the only good gook is a dead gook, then the only good Vietnamese is a dead Vietnamese, like if you could get away with it, you know, blow them away.

Dellums: Thank you.

Congresswoman Shirley Chisholm: I would like to ask you, on the basis of your testimony it would seem that the racism which is so inherent in the bloodstream of our nation in a very real sense was transported abroad and became a part of the total practices and training of our men for this war against the so-called gooks.

In other words, what I am saying is that it is not only a question of what has happened in Vietnam, but it is also a question of a total overall foreign policy and racial policy toward people. And would you say that seems to be the overall philosophy?

Campbell: Well, I do not know about the overall foreign policy, but I know in Indochina that is the idea, you know that they are inferior to us, and that pretty well sums it up. When you go into combat and you have got a rifle in your hands and you believe every slant-eye around you is inferior, you are not exactly going to treat them with kid gloves.

"Gook" became forever tied to one of the most disturbing wars in American history. The United States attempted to "save Vietnam from Communism" by killing hundreds of thousands of Vietnamese civilians, among whom were embedded the Vietcong and North Vietnamese Army. As was the case with the conquest of the Philippines and the occupation of Haiti, the United States utilized morally reprehensible methods. But in Vietnam, the United States employed a new method of war. The "carpet bombing" of civilian and military targets with conventional weapons, the "sticky fire" known as napalm, and chemical weapons like the foliage–destroyer Agent Orange often killed civilians indiscriminately. American bombers sometimes flew many times over the same area to ensure that it was completely leveled.

Although the U.S. had used concentration camps in the Philippines, none were built in Vietnam; the Nazi concentration camps may have caused that method to fall out of favor. The U.S. stated explicitly that the Vietnam War was a war of attrition, and the goal was not the gaining of territory mile by mile, but rather killing so many of the enemy that that enemy eventually gives up. In the end, millions of Vietnamese were killed in both South Vietnam and North Vietnam, a major portion of them having been civilians killed by American bombing.

The racist term "gook" was brought back to the United States by hundreds of thousands of Vietnam veterans. But not all those veterans repeated the epithet. After all, "gook" was a racist term.

Those who wished to speak of those enemy soldiers they faced in the field often used the slang "V.C." or "Charlie." One African American veteran remembered how some white veterans returned from Vietnam using the term "gook" to refer to the Vietnamese, but, as he put it, "the brothers didn't." African American veterans refused to say "gook" and only used "Charlie," because they saw the word "gook" as no different from "nigger." Incidentally, this veteran hailed from a town close to my hometown, and his family, like mine, had been terrorized by the KKK.

The dehumanization of people by labeling them "gooks" or "niggers" is not unusual or unique to American military activities. The Japanese Imperial Army had words similar to "gook" to describe the Koreans and Chinese as they killed them indiscriminately during World War II. The Chinese and Koreans had their own demeaning labels for the Japanese. Terrorists identifying themselves as Muslims tend to speak of their targets as "infidels" or "Zionists." Iranian revolutionaries who took American hostages called the United States "the Great Satan."

The use of racist and dehumanizing terms is worldwide. During the Vietnam War, "gook" gained popular usage in the United States, and even here, the word has been associated with violence. I know this from my own experiences of being called a "gook." The racism fostered within the United States, then, bolsters the attitudes thought necessary for continuing U.S. military operations in foreign lands, completing a cycle of racism.

The likes of John McCain have played a crucial role in this cycle, sustaining racist language in the public discourse and injecting his racial attitudes into American foreign policy.

Chapter 02
Ten Principles of War

How can we identify when a group of people has been transformed into "gooks" within U.S. foreign policy? Here are some basic principles.

1. In order to help them, it may be necessary to kill large numbers of them. This concept became discussed widely during the Vietnam War, as it seemed that the United States was willing to obliterate Vietnam in order to save it from Communism. In fact, it seemed that destroying Vietnam was the only way that the United States was willing to "save" it, as the only other way of saving the nation was by launching a full-scale traditional ground invasion of North Vietnam. And that was too costly a commitment for the United States.

2. A corollary to principle #1. We, the United States, are primarily interested in "helping" this group of people by waging war in their nation. We are relatively uninterested in helping these people by providing food, shelter, or medicine. During the Vietnam War, the entire American economy was distorted in order to provide the material and labor needs of the two-decade American military intervention in Southeast Asia, starting with air support

for the French colonial war there in the early 1950s, to the last bullet fired between the Vietcong and a young American soldier in 1973. But when millions of Vietnamese refugees attempted in the late 1970s to escape from Communist Vietnam, it is said that perhaps as many as a million of them died on the open seas. Many of them sank in faulty ships. Many were raped and killed by pirates. A tiny fraction of the annual war budget could have been utilized to rescue all of these refugees. But such missions are boring, apparently.

3. It is morally acceptable to instigate a civil war in a nation of people considered "gooks." Whatever happens as a result of that war is the fault of the forces we consider the enemy. The State Department and the CIA knew that a U.S. invasion of Iraq may bring about a civil war between newly liberated armed groups in Iraq. The responsible organs of the U.S. government (outside of the president himself) knew of the simmering tensions between the Sunni, Shia, and Kurdish ethnic/religious groups. The ensuing civil war has cost the lives of hundreds of thousands of people. Nevertheless, no one in the U.S. government has taken responsibility for both the "quagmire" or the bloodbath that the U.S. is now refereeing. The stated implication is that all of this is the fault of the now–dead Saddam Hussein. Our collective conscience can be cleared, as the tragic deaths of civilians resulting from the American occupation can be blamed on Saddam Hussein, however dead he might be.

4. A corollary of principle #3. It is morally acceptable, and in fact, we may consider it our moral obligation to support the most morally reprehensible and violent parties in the "gook" nation in order for us to struggle for some larger cause. The larger "end" justifies the vile means.

5. There are explicit or unspoken reasons for why these people are not equal to us. These reasons may be racial, religious, cultural, or completely arbitrary in some other manner.

6. A corollary to principle #5. This racism, stereotyping, simplification and distortion of these people makes it easier for us to apply principles #1 to #4 to them.

7. Our desire or need to apply principles #1 to #4 against these people prompts us to create and propagate the racial and other stereotypes and caricatures developed as a result of principle #5.

8. When dealing with people considered "gooks," it is easier to twist our own belief systems in order to justify violence, murder, and torture. Even devout Christians, Jews, and Muslims develop "theories" justifying most wars. Of course, in most situations, these theories are mere excuses to roll out the cannons and start the killing. The "just war" theories of Christians remind one of the justification of violence for the purpose of "jihad." Whatever the justification, one question invariably avoided when warring with populations considered subhuman is: What would Jesus do?

9. As long as the stated purpose is to kill the enemy, it does not matter how many innocent children, women, and men in the vicinity are killed, maimed or tortured. Many of these people, of course, are not anywhere near the "enemy" when they are attacked purposefully or "by accident."

10. As a justification of #9, we consider it very difficult to tell the difference between the stated "enemy" and innocent civilians, between "military" targets and "civilian" targets. They all look the same, so to speak.

An eleventh principle is the psychological foundation of all ten principles: do not put yourself in the shoes of the "gook." Empathy must be avoided. Empathy transforms "gooks" into people.

But even empathy goes only so far in the fog of war.

Chapter 03
From Napalm to Nixon:
McCain in his Prime

At the age of thirty, John McCain was deployed by the U.S. Navy to Vietnam.

John McCain was a bomber pilot. His job was to drop bombs on people and buildings.

When "foot soldiers" recall fighting and killing other soldiers, they are often haunted by the faces of those buddies who died around them. Perhaps a buddy died in their arms. These soldiers are sometimes disturbed by the faces of those that they killed — shot, stabbed, slit. It does not matter the race of the other human being, when a soldier is face-to-face with the enemy, their humanity can make an impression.

The bomber pilot is generally spared this face-to-face confrontation.

In 1967, John McCain flew his first bombing mission over North Vietnam, as part of Operation Rolling Thunder. Robert McNamara estimated that during Operation Rolling Thunder, from 1965 to 1968, the U.S. dropped on Vietnam two to three times the tonnage of bombs it dropped on Western Europe during World War II. He estimated that one million people were killed or injured each year as a result of the U.S. bombing of Hanoi and rural areas. John McCain and the other bombers were indispensable to Operation Rolling Thunder.

There is little evidence that John McCain ever held regrets or doubts about bombing either military targets or civilians. Except for one moment of his life. This moment is apparently buried deep in McCain's psyche, as he has backed away from the emotional words he said directly after this terrible event.

On July 29, 1967, as McCain flew off on his sixth bombing mission from the aircraft carrier, *USS Forrestal*, an accidentally fired missile hit his plane's fuel tank. The plane caught fire, and then bombs sitting on the plane and aircraft carrier began exploding. McCain watched his buddies and comrades burn to death, the "sticky fire" of napalm frying their bodies. Some men jumped off the aircraft carrier into the ocean. The fires burned uncontrolled into the night before finally falling under the control of the sailors. The fires and explosions killed 134 men.

For perhaps the only time in his life, John McCain suffered some doubts as to whether an American military act was morally acceptable. Writes Robert Dreyfuss in *The Nation*:

> . . . sipping Scotch in a Saigon villa with Johnny Apple of the New York Times, McCain reflected on the trauma. "It's a difficult thing to say," he said, "but now that I've seen what the bombs and the napalm did to the people on our ship, I'm not so sure that I want to drop any more of that stuff on North Vietnam."

The confession was extraordinary. But these feelings did not overwhelm McCain. Weeks later, McCain volunteered again to fly bombing missions over Hanoi.

On October 26, 1967, McCain flew a bombing mission over a heavily populated area of Hanoi. His plane was shot down and he ejected. Badly injured after ejecting himself from the plane, he fell into a lake. By some accounts, he went under the water and was rescued by a North Vietnamese soldier named Mai Van On. Mai, with whom McCain would be later re-united under friendly terms, pulled McCain out of the water and protected him from angry civilians wanting to attack McCain.

Nevertheless, as McCain recalled in a 1973 *U.S. News & World Report* article, he was struck with a rifle butt and stabbed in the foot with a bayonet. McCain, one arm and one leg severely broken, was taken to the "Hanoi Hilton," as the U.S. soldiers called it. It was a POW prison infamous for its terrible conditions and the torture that prisoners suffered at the hands of prison guards. There, the condition of McCain's broken leg threatened his life, but he survived with aid from the prison doctors. McCain never fully regained complete range of motion of his arm and leg.

McCain was tortured many times during his five and a half years at the "Hanoi Hilton." He was beaten. He was forced to hold difficult positions for hours. According to McCain, one of the worst forms of torture was solitary confinement. Being unable to communicate with other American POWs was extremely difficult.

McCain's experience was worse than death. I truly believe that. I would have preferred death.

Because McCain was the son of a famous Navy commander, he was often given "special" treatment, meaning, he was offered his freedom if he would accept it. He refused to do so because military protocol required that POWs should be freed in the order of capture. Nevertheless, because he was the most famous POW in North Vietnam, many people came to visit McCain, including the top general of the North Vietnamese army. McCain's 1973 *U.S. News & World Report* article is almost certainly the first time he published the word "gook" in the mass media:

> After I had been there about 10 days, a "gook"—which is what we called the North Vietnamese—came in one morn- ing. This man spoke English very well. He asked me how I was, and said, "We have a Frenchman who is here in Hanoi visiting, and would like to take a message back to your

family." Being a little naïve at the time—you get smarter as you go along with these people—I figured this wasn't a bad deal at all, if this guy would come to see me and go back and tell my family that I was alive.

Please note here that McCain does not distinguish between his prison guards and other Vietnamese. They are all "gooks," according to McCain. McCain would later claim that he refers only to his "prison guards" as "gooks." McCain refers to a Vietnamese person as "gook" a total of twelve times in his *U.S. News* article.

McCain states that "we" called the North Vietnamese "gooks." It should be noted that not all American servicemen called the Vietnamese "gooks." There were tens of thousands of pro–U.S. soldiers from South Korea who likely grated at the epithet which was also used by American GIs against Koreans. Filipino American, Chinese American, Japanese American, and Hawaiian American soldiers also served in Vietnam. It's hard to imagine any of them calling anyone a "gook." Many whites and blacks also refused to use the racial epithet.

McCain says that "gook" was applied to the *North* Vietnamese. Perhaps McCain makes this distinction to make the reading more comfortable for the conservative readers of *U.S. News & World Report*. It was certainly more convenient to see the North Vietnamese as the bad guys and the South Vietnamese as the good guys. But in reality, the situation was much more complicated. The "enemy" included South Vietnamese Vietcong, South Vietnamese civilians supporting the Vietcong, South Vietnamese members of the Communist Party, and their supporters. That is why "gook" was applied to all Vietnamese, perhaps *especially* South Vietnamese, as American soldiers constantly encountered South Vietnamese on their search and destroy missions and also in non–combat situations.

If McCain called only the North Vietnamese "gooks," it seems to reveal in him a simplistic or distorted view of the war.

Most likely, the assertion that the North Vietnamese rather than the South Vietnamese were "gooks" simply provided an excuse to call Vietnamese people "gooks" in a popular national magazine. Here is another example near the end of McCain's article:

> By the way—a very interesting thing—after I got back [to the U.S.], Henry Kissinger told me that when he was in Hanoi to sign the final agreements, the North Vietnamese offered him one man that he could take back to Washington with him, and that was me. He, of course, refused, and I thanked him very much for that, because I did not want to go out of order. Most guys were betting that I'd be the last guy out — but you never can fathom the "gooks."

The last sentence here implies, "You can never fathom the nature of the Vietnamese." The Vietnamese are inscrutable, he implies. Here, the word "gook" seems to bolster his application of a racial stereotype. It is similar to his assertion earlier in the article that "The Oriental, as you may know, likes to beat around the bush quite a bit." In that instance, he refers to the Oriental *character*, our supposed stereotypical "Asian traits." The point is that for McCain, "gook" is synonymous with "Vietnamese."

Throughout the article, McCain refers to various people as "gooks." They are not all "prison guards." McCain wrote the article when he was 37 years old. It is curious that a 37 year-old man who proudly wore the Navy uniform was calling people "gooks" in a national magazine. In contrast, typical Vietnam veterans do not use the word "gook" in public, much less in the mass media. They know that it is as offensive as "nigger."

According to many who have written on McCain's life, he was an angry man before he served in Vietnam, and he remained an angry, easily enraged, man upon his return. As a child, his anger would cause him to faint. And even today, he has admitted that every morning he wakes up and tells himself to control his temper. He has had a habit of yelling at reporters and campaign workers, and going so far as physically attacking those people who disagree with him.

McCain suffered beatings, torture, malnutrition, solitary confinement, demoralizing propaganda, and disease in prison. At one point, McCain was tortured into signing a confession of war crimes. During the 2000 presidential campaign, George Bush's campaign "helpers" told South Carolinians that McCain had betrayed his nation.

McCain, though, has his own strict vision of what an American soldier must do in times of war and imprisonment. Near the end of his captivity, McCain and the other POWs witnessed President Nixon's renewed carpet bombing of Hanoi.

> Finally came the day I'll never forget—the eighteenth of December, 1972. The whole place exploded when the Christmas bombing ordered by President Nixon began. They hit Hanoi right off the bat.

> It was the most spectacular show I'll ever see. By then we had large windows in our rooms. These had been covered with bamboo mats, but in October, 1972, they took them down. We had about a 120-degree view of the sky, and, of course, at night you can see all the flashes. The bombs were dropping so close that the building would shake. The SAM's [surface-to-air missiles] were flying all over and the sirens were whining—it was really a wild scene. When a B-52 would get hit—they're up at more than 30,000 feet—it would light up the whole sky. There would be a red glow that almost made it like daylight, and it would last for a long time, because they'd fall a long way.

John McCain believed that America should obliterate North Vietnam in order to win the war. But this Christmas bombing campaign contradicted what President Nixon had promised to do in 1968 — end the war. It was four years later, and Nixon had only expanded the war into Cambodia and Laos. He had mined civilian harbors and renewed the bombing of the city of Hanoi. Amazingly, American allies became concerned about the massive numbers of civilian deaths resulting from the renewed bombing. Governments throughout Europe and even the Pope condemned the United States for its bombing campaign. The Vietnamese, it seemed, were considered human beings by people outside of the peace movement, and, as a result, some of the B–52 pilots ordered to bomb Hanoi refused to do so. Writes McCain:

> I have heard there was one B–52 pilot who refused to fly the missions during the Christmas bombing. You always run into that kind. When the going gets tough, they find out their conscience is bothering them. I want to say this to anybody in the military: If you don't know what your country is doing, find out. And if you find you don't like what your country is doing, get out before the chips are down.
>
> Once you become a prisoner of war, then you do not have the right to dissent, because what you do will be harming your country. You are no longer speaking as an individual, you are speaking as a member of the armed forces of the United States, and you owe loyalty to the Commander in Chief, not to your own conscience. Some of my fellow prisoners sang a different tune, but they were a very small minority. I ask myself if they should be prosecuted, and I don't find that easy to answer. It might destroy the very fine image the great majority of us have brought back from that hellhole. Remember, a handful of turncoats after the Korean War made a great majority of Americans think that most of the POW's in conflict were traitors.
>
> If these men are tried, it should not be because they took an antiwar stance, but because they collaborated with the Vietnamese to an extent, and that was harmful to the other American POW's. And there is this to consider: America will have other wars to fight until the Communists give up their doctrine of violent overthrow of our way of life. These men should bear some censure so that in future wars there won't be a precedent for conduct that hurts this country.

There's a bit of "my country right or wrong," in McCain's writing. Some may consider this an admirable trait for a soldier. After all, they are there to follow orders, not to think too much. But coming from a man who would never face combat again, it seems to indicate a rigid, simplistic worldview.

What makes it more disturbing is McCain's insistence, as the final American troops withdrew from Vietnam, that "America will have other wars to fight until the Communists give up their doctrine of violent overthrow of our way of life." First, neither Mao nor Brezhnev or Krushchev had ever composed a doctrine concerning the overthrow of the way of life in the United States, so McCain's assertion seemed to indicate that the U.S. would continue fighting wars for the duration of history.

Second, assuming that the United States have a choice as to whether it will engage in war, it is interesting that McCain assumes that the U.S. will choose to engage in further wars for the sake of combating Communism. He seems to be advocating for further war in his tone and language. Luckily for the people or our nation, U.S. elected officials did not feel the same way as McCain. The next major military operation of the United States would be Reagan's short–lived military incursion into Beirut, Lebanon in the early 1980s. After that the U.S. invaded the tiny nation of Granada, and after that there was the relatively easy but destructive and murderous invasion of Panama in 1989. In total, Americans killed in action between the end of the Vietnam War and the beginning of the first Persian Gulf War totaled in the hundreds. What would that total have been had McCain been President and continued his worldwide war against Communists?

Besides "my country, right or wrong" McCain seemed to also believe in "Nixon, right or wrong" or perhaps "the Republican Party, right or wrong":

> I admire President Nixon's courage. There may be criti-
> cism of him in certain areas—Watergate, for example. But
> he had to take the most unpopular decisions that I could
> imagine—the mining, the blockade, the bombing. I know
> it was very, very difficult for him to do that, but that was
> the thing that ended the war. I think the reason he un-
> derstood this is that he has a long background in dealing

with these people. He knows how to use the carrot and the stick. Obviously, his trip to China and the Strategic Arms Limitation Treaty with Russia were based on the fact that we're stronger than the Communists, so they were willing to negotiate. Force is what they understand. And that's why it is difficult for me to understand now, when everybody knows that the bombing finally got a cease-fire agreement, why people are still criticizing his foreign policy—for example, the bombing in Cambodia.

John McCain seemed to have an overriding need to make things simple for himself. Nixon is right, his critics are wrong. All of the policies that McCain defended turned out to be tremendous disasters or obvious contradictions to McCain's beliefs, and McCain refused to recognize that.

McCain seems to trivialize the Watergate scandal, which would result in the revelation of various crimes and dirty tricks conducted by the Nixon administration, for which Nixon would resign. McCain says that Nixon had to bomb, blockade and mine Vietnam in order to end the war. Nixon could have ended the war in 1969, with essentially the same peace agreement. No concessions were won through expanding the war over the next four years. It only prolonged McCain's imprisonment and increased the death toll on all sides of the war.

By expanding the bombing into Cambodia and by overthrowing the government there, the Nixon administration only ensured that the genocidal Maoist Communist group known as the Khmer Rouge would take control of the nation and kill another 1 to 3 million Cambodians.

McCain was a true believer in the domino theory. He implies that Communism is such a great evil that the United States must fight it militarily everywhere. He believes that a single country becoming Communist would cause one after another country to fall to Communist Parties and/or Communist armies around the world. Apparently, there were Communist forces all over the world ready to take over nations once the first one fell.

If this were the case, then should not the worst Communists be fought most violently? In 1972, the most murderous living Communist leader, Mao Tse Tung, was in the middle of destroying his nation through the Cultural Revolution and simultaneously aiding the North Vietnamese in their war against the United States.

And yet Nixon went to China to establish friendly relations in the middle of the Vietnam War. Millions of innocent people were killed as a result of the Cultural Revolution, but Nixon landed in Beijing as if Mao were the president of Canada. So here was Richard Nixon sending American young men to die in the war against Communism worldwide while simultaneously hanging out at Mao Tse Tung's home, saying things like, "There is no reason for us to be enemies. Neither of us seeks the territory of the other; neither of us seeks domination over the other; neither of us seeks to stretch out our hands and rule the world." But was not that why the United States was in Vietnam — because the Communists sought world domination? And was not the Chinese Communist Party seeking the "violent overthrow of our way of life"? After all, China's Communist government sent hundreds of thousands of Chinese soldiers and crucial military aid to the North Vietnamese Army.

It seems strange that while Nixon and Mao were toasting each other, drinking Chinese whiskey, walking from table to table in the banquet room, the Chinese government was at that moment sending more men, more guns, and more supplies to shoot down American planes and dig tunnels for the Vietcong.

But at age 37, McCain was still wearing blinders. He seemed to believe in the entire mythology of the Cold War. He believed, it seems, that there really was a good-versus-evil war between the United States and the Communist powers of the world and that that war was driven by principles of right and wrong. He embraced Richard Nixon as the great decider of what was right and what was wrong. While other Vietnam veterans returned to the United States confused and wondering how everything had gone so wrong in American government, McCain seemed to ignore all of the obvious contradictions and policy disasters of the Nixon machine and wonder publicly, "Why all the fuss over Nixon?"

John McCain's use of the epithet "gook" in the 1970s demonstrates more than his lack of political correctness. It signals a dangerous habit of simplifying the world into the rights of the right wing, and the wrongs of all others; the divine rights of "us" and the expendability of those foreign peoples whom we consider less than human.

Chapter 04
Does John McCain resent Martin Luther King, Jr.?

John McCain was 26 years old when Dr. Martin Luther King, Jr., gave his landmark speech, "I Have a Dream."

It is unclear what John McCain felt about Dr. King's vision. But it is clear what McCain's mentor and predecessor, Arizona Senator Barry Goldwater, felt about it. He wanted to keep the Dream just that, a dream.

The Dream represented the *true* declaration of independence of our nation. Yes, the 1776 declaration mentioned that "all men are created equal." But the Dream speech declared that we, the people, would make equality *a reality*. Dr. King explicitly stated that Americans were demanding our nation make good on that promise of equality.

And if the Dream speech was a "Declaration," then the Civil Rights Act of 1964 and the Voting Rights Act of 1965 were the new, *true* U.S. Constitution, Emancipation Proclamation, and first fourteen amendments of the Constitution. After all, the human rights outlined in the original Constitution applied only to some Americans and excluded African Americans.

The twelfth through fourteenth amendments recognized the political and civil rights of African Americans, but those rights were not enforced. They were in many ways meaningless.

The passage of the Civil Rights Act and the Voting Rights Act finally gave meaning to the previous documents and amendments, as these Acts marked the first *sincere* attempt by America to become *America.*

Goldwater was a paragon of right-wing politics for McCain to emulate. Goldwater mentored McCain and even ran McCain's campaign to fill Goldwater's senate seat. Senator Goldwater voted against *both* the Civil Rights Act and the Voting Rights Act. Most senators in 1964 and 1965 did not think the same way as Barry Goldwater. If they did, people of color in the South would still be unable to vote and Americans of color would still attend segregated schools. We would drink at segregated water fountains, and certain groups would sit in the backs of buses and would not be allowed in restaurants. For most of us in today's world, Goldwater's vision for America is a nightmare.

In 1998, McCain wrote a tribute to Goldwater wherein McCain seems to defend Goldwater's attempt to keep things the way they were — racist, segregated and anti-American. Writes McCain:

> When we recall Barry Goldwater's long and distinguished career, we are reminded of the best attributes of a public servant. A great person's biography is marked by consistency, integrity and lasting achievement. Such was the life and career of Barry Goldwater. He held his principles close to his heart, where he held his love of country. He lived his public and private lives according to those principles, and woe to the miscreant who ran afoul of them. He always rushed to defend his ground, whether or not the ground he defended was in fashion at the time.
>
> The changes in political attitudes that occur regularly in any nation's history often weaken the resolve of ordinary statesmen. But extraordinary statesmen do not let the

vagaries of public opinion impair their vision or weaken their heart. ("Barry Goldwater, Patriot and Politician" by John McCain, *Washington Post*, 5/30/1998)

According to McCain, "changes in political attitudes" occurred in America and Goldwater's views were no longer "in fashion," but he nevertheless "defended his ground" against the "miscreants" who trespassed upon his "principles." Among those principles Goldwater defended were the segregation and subjugation of black people. Goldwater's desperate grip on the remnants of an old, segregated America was one of the "best attributes of a public servant," according to McCain.

Or was it? Let us look for more clues as to how McCain really felt.

Goldwater's backwards attitude cost him the 1964 presidential election, which he lost to the pro–civil rights candidate, Lyndon B. Johnson. Certainly, though, the 1965 Voting Rights Act was not the end of the ongoing struggle for equality and dignity in the United States.

Important to the continuing civil rights movement was the struggle for a Martin Luther King holiday. Celebrating MLK Day allows Americans each year to renew their dedication to realizing the most beautiful vision of America ever conceived by a major American leader. Just as July 4th celebrates the independence of the United States, MLK Day celebrates the nonviolent American revolution for human rights and human dignity.

John McCain held his ground. In 1983, John McCain was one of a small minority of Congressmen to vote against establishing Martin Luther King Day. While the federal MLK holiday was passed over the objections of McCain and others, the states had to decide then if they were going to implement their own MLK holidays.

With the help of a Democratic governor, Arizona did just that. But in 1987, Arizona inaugurated Republican Governor Evan Mecham. He immediately rescinded the state's Martin Luther King Holiday. Although this was an issue of *state* law, John McCain, a U.S. senator, expressed his opposition to Martin Luther King Day to teenagers in Phoenix. According to the *Washington Post*, "McCain said that he felt Mecham was correct in rescinding the holiday."

I wonder what it was like to be a child listening to my famous senator tell me that getting rid of Martin Luther King Day was the right thing to do. I would have been heartbroken and alienated.

A corruption scandal forced Evan Mecham to resign, and a nationwide campaign pressured Arizona to reinstate the MLK holiday. By the time Public Enemy released their scorching "By the time I get to Arizona," McCain had caved in to popular sentiment. The "enormous proportions" of the issue forced McCain to support an MLK *state* holiday, but not a federal holiday: "I'm still opposed to another federal holiday... but I support the (Arizona) Martin Luther King holiday *because of the enormous proportions this issue has taken on as far as the image of our state* and our treatment towards not only blacks but all minorities." True to his beliefs, in 1994 McCain voted against funding the federal Martin Luther King Holiday Commission, which had been established in 1984 to oversee the implementation of the holiday.

While the nation struggled over MLK Day, newly appointed Supreme Court justices were rolling back civil rights legislation and precedent. In 1990, a new civil rights bill was aimed at restoring the civil rights precedents lost during the Reagan–Bush years. According to Sam Stein:

> The act was a response to a series of controversial Supreme Court decisions made the year before. In those decisions, the court overturned a 1971 ruling that required employers to prove a "business necessity" for screening out minorities and women in its hiring practices. That burden of proof, the 1989 court said, should instead be placed on the plaintiff who alleged that his or her client had been unlawfully screened.

> Both the House of Representatives and the Senate, deeming this unjust, passed bills that would restore the old law. But the Bush administration objected, insisting that a reversion to the old way would amount to forcing employers to have hiring quotas. It was a controversial and somewhat dubious claim, one that the New York Times editorial

page called "an unjustified charge." After all, the system had worked fine from 1971 through 1989. Nevertheless, the president vetoed the legislation.

When a motion to override the veto came to the Senate floor, there was question as to whether it would receive the 67 votes needed to pass. The environment was so charged that white supremacist David Duke watched from one section of the Senate gallery while civil rights leader Jesse Jackson stood briefly at the chamber's other end.

The Civil Rights Act needed only *one more vote* to pass the Senate. Did Barry Goldwater whisper in McCain's ear, or did McCain vote his heart? McCain struck the bill down, and it died in the Senate.

While McCain boasts of his reputation for bucking against the Republican Party, when it comes to civil rights, McCain walks in lockstep with the farthest-right feather of the far-right wing of the Republican Party.

On MLK Day 2007, John McCain attended as a special "guest" Republican Bob Riley's inauguration as the governor of Alabama. At the time, Riley was being criticized for belonging to an all-white organization. The Grand Master of the Grand Lodge of Alabama admitted to the Associated Press in 2006 that out of 30,000 members, none were black.

Who is the true "Grand Master"? McCain fought against MLK Day, and upon giving in to popular sentiment, he still opposed enforcing the civil rights legislation Dr. King died for. Does John McCain embrace Dr. King's dream of equality? Or does McCain reluctantly accept an MLK holiday as a "necessary evil" on his path to the White House?

Who is the true John McCain?

Chapter 05
We can still win
the Vietnam War.

John McCain cannot leave Vietnam.

By 1998, John McCain had served as a Congressman and Senator for sixteen years, and had passed his fifty-first birthday. One would hope that he had superseded Barry Goldwater's mindset as the end of the millennium drew near. But McCain seemed stuck in the Goldwater/George Wallace mindset of 1964–1968. According to Robert Dreyfuss writing in a January 2000 article in *The Nation*, McCain stuck to his belief that the United States could have and should have bombed Vietnam into submission:

> McCain expanded on this theme in a speech to the American Bar Association on the thirtieth Anniversary of the 1968 Tet Offensive by North Vietnam and the Viet Cong. "Like a lot of Vietnam veterans, I believed and still believe that the war was winnable," he said. "I do not believe that it was winnable at an acceptable cost in the short or probably long term using the strategy of attrition which we em-

ployed there to such tragic results. I do believe that had we taken the war to the North and made full consistent use of air power in the North, we ultimately would have prevailed."

How much more bombing does John McCain want? Let's say we use massive bombing to destroy all of Hanoi and every major city. Let's say we bomb all the rice fields so that the NVA cannot eat, and neither can the people. Let's say we drop nuclear bombs on the necessary cities. And then we send in ground troops to handle the survivors. Would that satisfy John McCain? Or perhaps he prefers carrying out bombing missions only until we've reached our moral limit — perhaps when the body count hits twenty million. And if we have "won" by then, God bless America.

Apparently, McCain still believes that it is proper to "annihilate a nation in order to save it." This peculiar notion was made popular during the Vietnam War, a war that John McCain seems to continue fighting, year after year.

Roger Simon of *U.S. News & World Report* was the first to report on McCain's use of the racial epithet "gook." McCain was telling a story from his time in a North Vietnamese POW prison. In this story, McCain had been working on a theatrical version of Charles Dickens' *A Christmas Carol* for the prisoners to act out. But, McCain explains, "the goddamn gooks came into the cell and took three of my stars out!" Wrote Simon:

> Strictly speaking, one does not say 'gooks' anymore. It is simply not done. But John McCain says 'gooks,' and who is going to tell him not to? And when he starts another story, talking about how he fell in love with one of the camp cooks and is asked what "his" name was, McCain says, "Please! It was a female! I never got *that* bad!"

> Strictly speaking, McCain might want to avoid that joke, considering Barney Frank once called him "a thousand percent anti-gay."

In *Divided We Stand*, a book on the 2000 presidential campaign, Roger Simon explains:

I was not the first journalist to hear McCain use the word "gooks," but I was the first to print it in a piece that appeared in U.S. News & World Report on September 27, 1999. My rule was simple: if the candidate says it, I report it. There is no journalistic justification for protecting a presidential candidate from himself.

So McCain, on the campaign trail 1998–2000, was talking of "gooks" on a regular basis well before September, 1999. How often did he utter the word?

I emailed Mr. Simon to ask him how often John McCain referred to Vietnamese as "gooks" and exactly whom he was calling "gooks." Simon did not respond to my email. If the person who wrote the "definitive" book on the 2000 presidential campaign cannot give me an answer, we can only look for clues to McCain's behavior in the works of other reporters who followed him on the campaign trail.

Sadly, reporters from the UK did a better job than U.S. reporters on covering McCain's use of this racial slur. Ben Macintyre of London's *The Times* reported in Washington, D.C. on December 11, 1999:

> A conservative politician who has cleverly cultivated and charmed the liberal US media, Mr McCain gets away with the sort of remarks that would blast a hole in any other candidate. Barely a hair is turned when he refers to the Vietnamese as "gooks", enumerates "one of the many reasons I hate the French" or makes insensitive jokes about Chelsea Clinton's looks and Alzheimer's disease ("You get to hide your own Easter eggs".)

On December 12, a book review of McCain's *Faith of my Fathers* in *The Observer* seems to mock McCain's free use of the racial slur:

> Signs up to fight the 'gooks' in Asia. Shot down, ejects, lands on water, pounced upon by gooks (picture included), taken prisoner.

Ed Vulliamy of *The Observer* commented on American journalists' attitude towards McCain:

> You see the journalists trying to shut him [McCain] up for his own sake. To him, the Vietcong are still 'Commie gooks'.

On December 19, *The Sunday Times* of London published a long feature on McCain which gushed over his obstinate machismo:

> For the feminised 1990s, McCain is refreshingly macho and direct, calling a fellow Republican senator a "f* jerk" and the heartthrob actor Leonardo DiCaprio "an androgynous wimp". Asked whether he had discussed drugs with his children, he replied that he had warned his 13–year–old son off by telling him "I'd beat him within an inch of his life". He still calls the Vietnamese "gooks", and described a minor diplomatic incident as "one of the many reasons why I hate the French".

Indeed, reporters from Europe seemed to feel much freer in their critiques of McCain. Wrote a Dublin writer in the *Sunday Business Post:*

> On other occasions, his loose tongue has got him into trouble. He has often used the racial slur "gook" to describe the Vietnamese, once admitting that "I'll hate those bastards for as long as I live".

Dreyfuss's landmark article in *The Nation* did not seem to cause McCain to pause in his sneering racial epithets. Published in the print edition on January 3, 2000, Dreyfuss demonstrated that the new millennium was identical to the old millennium and described McCain as a man who resembles both: "scary."

> Perhaps the most striking example of the media's unwillingness to challenge McCain's air of moral authority is when he shocks listeners by casually calling the

Vietnamese "gooks." ... A quarter of a century [after returning from the war], while speaking with reporters aboard the Straight Talk Express in October, McCain was still calling Vietnamese "gooks" —and according to a reporter who was there, no one called him on it.

Despite *The Nation's* respected place among journalists, the article made exactly zero impact on the American media's continued protection of McCain's image and political well-being.

AN ETHICAL ISSUE

What American reporter had the guts to quote John McCain using the word "gook"? Of the dozens of reporters who likely heard McCain speak of "gooks," only one reporter dared quote McCain saying "gook" in the months or years leading up to February 17, 2000. Of all the times McCain referred to Vietnamese persons as "gooks" and did so "for the record" from 1973 to February 17, 2000, only Roger Simon quoted him.

And even then, Simon implanted the quote in a story about the maverick mouth of John McCain. The fact that John McCain was, on a regular basis, spitting out this racial epithet as if it were the score to last night's game *deserved a story of its own.* A cover story on each of the major news weeklies, above the fold headlines on the major dailies, and lead stories in the evening news would have been appropriate.

In 2006, Republican Senator George Allen called a man a "macaca," a derogatory term used against blacks in North Africa. The man that Allen was insulting was of South Asian descent. Heavy media coverage of Allen's "macaca" comment essentially killed Allen's political career, even though he was being hailed as a Republican presidential candidate.

American journalists dashed Jesse Jackson's presidential hopes in 1984 when they reported repeatedly Jackson's reference to New York as "Hymietown." H. Ross Perot received tremendous negative coverage for using the phrase "you people" while speaking to the NAACP in 1992.

In the 2008 election, reporters have spent thousands of hours doing frame–by–frame analyses of the sermons of Rev. Jeremiah Wright to dissect them for possibly racist or paranoid content. Imagine if Barack Obama's former pastor had called a white person a "cracker." How many weeks of coverage would that have consumed on the major news networks?

But this hypothetical is not exactly analogous. Wright is a presidential candidate's ex–pastor, while John McCain is *the presidential candidate himself.*

What if *Barack Obama* had said the word "cracker" in reference to a white person? His campaign would be over in an instant. If *Hillary Clinton* had referred to a Mexican as a "spic," her political career would have been buried. In both cases, journalists would have recorded exactly what was said, how it was said, why it was said, what the context was, what the intended meaning was, what the possible interpretations of the words were, what the political ramifications might be, and so forth. Journalists would have interviewed on national television various national leaders of the respective ethnic or racial groups. And every time either of the Democratic candidates *repeated* the racial epithet, the pundits and reporters would have slammed them over and over. People like George Will would have written numerous columns. Sunday news shows would have spent months grilling the culprits and their supporters.

John McCain utters "gook" over the course of at least seven months and perhaps over a period of twenty–seven years, and reporters offer one quote, reluctantly, buried in a story about McCain's maverick mouth, featuring McCain sporting flashy sunglasses.

It is an issue of ethics.

Journalists have an *ethical obligation* to report accurately and in detail the actions and wrongdoings of the elected officials of the United States. If Richard Nixon was using the word "nigger" or "kike," it was the obligation of journalists to report exactly how he was doing so, and journalists did act ethically and emphatically, when it came to Nixon. The detailed investigative reporting on Nixon's many crimes against the nation and against humanity demonstrated the ability of American journalists to analyze complex conspiracies powerful people hoped to bury.

In Nixon's case, reporters continued to report on his racism even after he had resigned, and then even after his death.

To purposefully give a presidential candidate preferential treatment is completely unethical. What is more incredible is that the journalists who have covered McCain's presidential campaigns have been some of the best paid and most highly regarded journalists in the nation. They work for some of the most popular periodicals and TV news programs in America. By not reporting McCain's "gook" comments precisely and immediately, these journalists are in essence reporting false news. That is, they have intentionally provided an incomplete image of a presidential candidate when we have every expectation as Americans to receive complete information from our most respected wielders of the free press.

Americans cannot trust the national press to report accurately on John McCain. They are highly biased in his favor. While McCain's racial attitudes are of utmost importance, we can only assume that we are missing some or most of the story.

Dreyfuss's *Nation* article demonstrated that McCain's habit of using racist epithets was an old habit which he partakes in shamelessly. Asian American leaders did read this important work, and responded. Sadly, out of a habitual shyness on the part of these Asian American leaders, they did not demand that McCain *withdraw from the presidential race.*

The statements Asian American leaders issued lacked boldness. Furthermore, those statements were issued to the same press that Karen Narasaki of National Asian Pacific American Legal Consortium explicitly blamed for "letting" McCain "get away with it." If the press cannot be trusted, then why rely on them?

An email criticizing McCain was also circulated.

Chapter 06
White Supremacists,
John McCain,
and the Southern Cross

By February 2000, John McCain was sitting pretty in the catbird seat. He had shocked the world by taking the New Hampshire primary by a wide margin over George W. Bush. And now he was campaigning in South Carolina with all the swagger of a cowboy riding a bucking maverick straight into the town square of Columbus, South Carolina.

Six-shooters blazing.

McCain's flaunting of the word "gook" hurt him not one bit in New Hampshire. So, McCain *only gained more confidence in saying and doing what he really, truly wanted to say and do.*

McCain seemed to enjoy the media coverage of his "zingers," as he continued to provide them for the record. Ian Bruce of Glasgow's *The Herald* wrote on February 5, 2000:

> In an era of political correctness, he still refers to the Vietnamese as "gooks", describes actor Leonardo DiCaprio as "an androgynous wimp", and admits that the anti-drugs

advice he imparted to his 13-year-old son was that if he caught him using them, he would "beat the shit out of him".

McCain let himself speak freely. He had been telling a story on the campaign trail about an Al Gore fund-raising event at a Buddhist temple in Los Angeles. In Fort Mill, South Carolina (conveniently he did this here rather than in California) he told the story and called the Asian monks "all those funny looking people in robes." This revealing quote was reported by the *Houston Chronicle* on February 18, and, of course, McCain was given the benefit of the doubt. If he had not been leading a months-long festival of racial epithets against those "funny-looking people," he may have actually deserved the benefit of the doubt.

MCCAIN'S MAIN MAN IN THE SOUTH

Richard Quinn is a lifelong white supremacist, meaning he has been a vigorous organizer of racist activities. In the old days, white supremacists gathered in the woods and burned crosses. Today, they carry descriptors like "neo-Confederate" and influence elections. Quinn has served as a Republican political consultant for politicians as crowded on the right-wing of that party as Ronald Reagan and segregationist Strom Thurmond. He received praise from segregationist John Ashcroft.

In 1979, the quarterly *Southern Partisan* was born. By 1983, Richard Quinn had become the Editor-In-Chief of the anti-black, anti-immigrant, anti-gay journal. Quinn had been born in North Carolina, and he seemed to spend his life trying to live down the fact that his birthplace was north of the Mason-Dixon Line.

By the time John McCain hired Richard Quinn, he and the *Southern Partisan* had long ago earned a reputation for publishing disgusting, racist essays costumed as intellectual "journal articles." One of the common themes of the *Southern Partisan* was essentially that slavery was not wrong:

> "Neither Jesus nor the apostles nor the early church condemned slavery, despite countless opportunities to

do so, and there is no indication that slavery is contrary to Christian ethics or that any serious theologian before modern times ever thought it was." — *Southern Partisan*, Third Quarter, 1995

"Slave owners... did not have a practice of breaking up slave families. If anything, they encouraged strong slave families to further the slaves' peace and happiness." — *Southern Partisan*, First Quarter, 1996

The *Southern Partisan* compared the first Grand Wizard of the Ku Klux Klan to a "superhero." The journal published a story about a slave that defended his master from Northerners trying to lynch him. It called feminism "a revolt against God." It called AIDS "a sign of God's wrath." The journal implied that Nelson Mandela was a "bad egg" while praising KKK candidate David Duke as a "maverick" (McCain's moniker). The journal wrote about Martin Luther King leading his people to the promised land of welfare. The *Southern Partisan* described Miami as "a city 56 percent Spanish-speaking that includes not only Cubans but numbers of cocaine-pushing trigger-happy Colombians." With Patrick Buchanan serving at one time as a "senior adviser," it's no surprise that the *Southern Partisan* had ties with the leading Holocaust-denial journal, *The Journal of Historical Review*.

It's not clear when John McCain first hired Richard Quinn as a Republican strategist. Certainly it was well before February 2000. Richard Quinn took on the role of McCain's chief strategist in South Carolina, and John McCain established his campaign headquarters in the same building as the *Southern Partisan*. Others in the building, which Quinn owned, were the Southern Heritage Foundation, which was heading the fight to keep the Confederate flag as the state symbol and the local chapter of the Sons of Confederate Veterans, which McCain was eligible to join (more on that later). Part of the hundreds of thousands (or millions) of dollars that McCain has paid to Richard Quinn over the years likely went to paying for the use of this haven for white supremacy.

Richard Quinn was one of the most prominent leaders of the Heritage Movement attempting to keep the Confederate flag flying above the South Carolina statehouse.

"Heritage" became the key word in the fight over the Confederate flag. Over the decades, over 500 hate groups and white supremacist groups have adapted the flag as their *"symbol of heritage."*

In 1962, the Confederate flag was adapted as the official flag of South Carolina by an all–white legislature. Since then, other Southern states removed the flag in part out of respect for the people of color living in their states. South Carolina refused to stop flying the Southern Cross. For most people of color in South Carolina, the Confederate flag, also known as the Confederate battle flag, represented a glorification of the days of Dixie — that is, the Confederate flag reminded them of one of the bloodiest systems of human slavery and subjugation the world has ever seen.

In order to pressure the state to take the battle flag down from its statehouse, the NAACP in 1999 implemented a boycott of the state, asking associations to organize their conventions in states other than South Carolina. It was a last resort for the NAACP, as their constituency had suffered the indignity of living under the Confederate flag for 37 years. In January 2000, in retaliation, South Carolina state senator Arthur Ravenal defended the Confederate flag and referred to the NAACP as the "National Association of Retarded People." He then apologized to "retarded people" for associating them with the African American organization. Ravenal was roundly criticized throughout the nation for his hateful comments.

Here comes John McCain to the rescue. Just days after Ravenal's comments, McCain cleared up conflicting statements he'd made concerning the Confederate battle flag. On January 11, just days before Martin Luther King Day, McCain stated, "As to how I view the flag, I understand both sides. Some view it as a symbol of slavery; others view it as a symbol of heritage. Personally, I see the battle flag as a *symbol of heritage.*"

Symbol of heritage, huh? Was it coincidence that John McCain was using the same language that white supremacists used to express their reverence for the Confederacy and old Dixieland? Was it accident that McCain's language indicated that McCain supported a return to the days of old? That he sought for the continued political, social, and economic domination of African Americans at the hands of the white elite? Ask yourself this. Was it accidental that John McCain hired a white supremacist to organize his campaign? Was it accidental that McCain shared a building with white supremacists and walked past them in the hall? Was it coincidence that McCain went to a headquarters of white supremacy to consort, consult, and organize with a leading white supremacist?

Richard Quinn, acting as McCain's spokesperson, clarified for reporters that the one time McCain called the Confederate flag offensive, he meant that it was offensive "to some people." Quinn also said — and this was confirmed by reporters — that McCain had *often* said that the Confederate flag was a symbol of heritage.

McCain's support was a great boon for the white supremacy movement, offering legitimacy to a fringe philosophy traditionally associated with KKK terrorism. Wrote *The Nation* on August 29, 2006:

> Before the [South Carolina] primary, Quinn organized a rally of 6,000 people in support of flying the Confederate flag over the statehouse. Quinn dressed up McCain volunteers in Confederate Army uniforms as they passed fliers to the demonstrators assuring them that McCain supported the Confederate flag.

For his part, McCain defended Quinn, saying that he was not a racist and refused to fire him despite pressure to cut ties with the anti–black activist. In 2008, Richard Quinn is still a well-paid strategist for McCain.

With John McCain leading the charge for the Confederate flag, people like Ravenal and Quinn were validated and legitimized, and their causes were illuminated with the halo of McCain's "maverick" nature. The Ku Klux Klansmen must have been dancing in their sheets, so to speak. When Martin Luther King Day rolled around, writers throughout the nation decried a "Banner Year for Racists," as Jonathan Yardley of the *Washington Post* called it. He asked on January 17: "Just how much is the Republican nomination worth [to John McCain]? Is it worth currying the favor of racists?" Yardley seemed to miss the point, and it is a point that has been missed for decades. It is a question that is ignored even today, as McCain prepares to win the Oval Office, and as TV pundits insist that "McCain does not have a racist bone in his body." Does not McCain by his actions prove that he does have a few racist bones in his body? That his racism may run as deep as his marrow?

By his actions, John McCain is a racist and a powerful, active racist.

Even the Southern *St. Petersburg Times* of Florida called Richard Quinn a Neo-Confederate and called for South Carolina to lower the Confederate flag in a January 21, 2000 editorial. If heritage is so important, the argument went, what about *black* Southern heritage? The Southern Cross does not represent black Southern heritage and represents, traditionally (and tradition is what counts here, right?), a *threat* to blacks and their heritage.

McCain is at least fifty years behind the times. That is, fifty years ago, he should have been fighting to *lower* the Confederate flag from state capitols. Instead, in the new millennium, he was fighting to keep the offensive symbol flying over the heads of people who find it disgusting and disturbing but are forced to abide by it.

Why did McCain fight against the efforts of the NAACP to turn the page on the Civil War? Why did McCain side with those who wished to keep the South mired in a Civil War mindset? McCain claimed, as stated before, that it was a symbol of heritage for Southerners, even though it was only right-wing whites that typically embraced it. But McCain also said that the flag represented his *own heritage.* For weeks, he spoke proudly of his Southern heritage and the fact that his "ancestors" fought for the Confederate flag during the Civil War. "Personally, I see the battle flag as a symbol of heritage. I have ancestors who have fought for the Confederacy, none of whom owned slaves. I believe they fought honorably."

But how does one fight honorably for the Confederacy? How does one fight honorably for the right to own, use, rape, beat, breed, sell, and work to death human beings? Even the rules of war do not allow for slavery. One cannot honorably, even according to the rules of war, enslave other soldiers. One cannot torture other soldiers. How can one honorably do these things to civilians?

Anyone trying to defend the Confederacy will contradict themselves unless they truly believe in the institution of slavery. McCain presumably does not believe in slavery, and neither did his ancestors own slaves. This is clear, as he repeated it to the American public, over and over. His ancestors fought honorably to prolong the Black Holocaust ad infinitum but did not own slaves themselves.

Except that his grandpa's grandpa did own slaves. William Alexander McCain owned 52 slaves. He owned little babies. He owned full-grown adults. And he even owned elderly people. McCain not only owned slaves, he also fought as a Confederate soldier to continue owning human beings.

John McCain's cousin, Elizabeth Spencer, writes openly about the family's slaves in her family memoir, *Landscapes of the Heart*. John McCain read this book while researching his own family memoir, *Faith of my Fathers*.

McCain portrays himself as a student of history, but he apparently chooses to ignore some parts of history and stress others. On February 15, McCain was confronted on his family's slave ownership. William McCain owned slaves, reporters told McCain. McCain said that he did not know this information. His advisers said that although McCain had read his cousin's memoir in order to write his own memoir, he had not read the family memoir very carefully. Knowing that William McCain owned a substantial plantation and knowing that William McCain fought for the Confederacy, John McCain assumed that he must *not* have owned slaves.

And then he passed off to the world as *truth* what he only *assumed*.

John McCain admitted to reporters that he "just hadn't thought about it," but that "it shouldn't be a surprise" that William McCain owned slaves. "They had a plantation and they fought in the Civil War so I guess that makes sense."

Here are some unanswerable questions for John McCain. How does McCain read a family memoir about his own family and miss the references to his family's slaves? Why didn't other members of the McCain family inform John that he was telling untruths to the public as he stomped across the South rallying the citizenry around the Confederate flag?

To borrow from Kanye West, does John McCain "care about black people"? If John McCain had one iota of emotional connection with black people, it seems he would have wondered if William McCain, who owned a plantation and fought for the Confederacy, owned slaves.

He would have asked other family members. He would have read the family memoir more carefully. He would have told an intern to find out.

White people who have deep roots in the South invariably ask their families, "Did we ever own slaves?" It is simply common thinking. Some people ask out of curiosity, others to honor some obligation to history and America. Many people do research to answer this question. It is simply something that Americans with some sense of connection and reverence for the grand and complex story of the American people ask about.

Yet McCain had no interest in his family's role in the four hundred year tragedy of slavery and exploitation. Although McCain is a well-known history buff, he had no interest in finding out if his family owned slaves.

This holocaust, it seems, was not important to McCain. It was trivial.

John McCain says he "just hadn't thought about it." It is as if, like Richard Quinn might put it, slavery was not that bad for African Americans, so why bother thinking about? Perhaps that statement is too harsh, or perhaps, deep in John McCain's heart, he just doesn't care much... about black people.

Chapter 07
"I hate the gooks."

Sometimes, it serves a larger purpose to be mean-spirited, malicious, and full of rage.

But those times tend to be when one is fighting for the well-being of people and animals. Not when one is fighting for one's right to hurt millions of people by continuing to use a racial epithet in the mass media.

February 17, 2000. According to Knight-Ridder reporters Steven Thomma and Ben Stocking in an article entitled, "McCain is defiant about his use of anti-Asian term," John McCain was being interviewed on his Straight Talk Express bus.

He was being interviewed about his "gook" comments. Circulating about the internet was an email that "complains" about McCain using "disparaging, racist remarks about Vietnamese people." McCain's response to hearing about this email was snappy and lacking in consideration or thought: "I'll call, right now, my interrogator that tortured me and my friends a gook, OK, and you can quote me." He also said, "In case it escaped somebody's notice, they were cruel, mean, vicious, sometimes sadistic people. And 'gook' is the kindest description I can give them, the most printable."

McCain's conversation with the reporters was then interrupted by a phone call. He conducted an unrelated interview on the phone for some time. He hung up the phone. McCain then turned to the reporters and said to them, "I hated the gooks, and I will hate them for as long as I live."

While the Knight–Ridder reporters published the most detailed account of McCain's meltdown concerning his "gook" comments, many other papers also reported the story. Reporters had finally decided that this was a story.

Terry M. Neal and Edward Walsh of the *Washington Post* offered the following documentation of McCain's words:

> "If anybody doesn't believe that these interrogators and these prison guards who tortured me and my friends were not cruel and sadistic people that deserve the appellation gook…. There's no appellation that could be bad enough. I'm referring to our prison guards," he said. "I will continue to refer to them probably in language that might offend some people here… I hated the gooks and will continue to hate them as long as I live."

It is important to note that some respectable news sources, such as the *San Francisco Chronicle*, quoted McCain as saying, "I *hate* the gooks. I will *hate* them as long as I live." He spoke in the present tense. All sources quoted McCain saying that he would hate "the gooks" until his death. Considering the multiple versions of McCain's expression of hate, it is unclear if he said he hated "the gooks" just once or multiple times.

Whatever the case, McCain wanted badly to be president. So badly, that he would do what it took to avoid controversy. According to the *Washington Times*, after his declaration of hate,

> Mr. McCain stood by his use of the word. "You can view that as a misstep if you want to. I'll call sadists and murderers a

lot worse than that." But he also said he would stop using the term "because I don't want to feel the fire."

A CURVATURE OF THE TRUTH

John McCain has a history of bending the truth.

According to the brilliant book *Free Ride: John McCain and the Media,* when reporters first approached McCain about his unethical relationship with Savings & Loan criminal Charles Keating, McCain claimed that they were "liars." When they offered some evidence of their charges, he was the one who seemed like the liar.

John McCain received hundreds of thousands of dollars in donations and free trips from Charles Keating in exchange for McCain's influence in the U.S. Senate, which was responsible for regulating Keating's savings and loan bank. McCain and four others, known as the Keating Five, organized a special meeting with those regulators to try to influence them. While three of the Keating Five were punished harshly, McCain walked away with a slap on the wrist.

Throwing the rest of the senators under the bus, McCain claimed that *he* was not asking any favors for Keating. But the Keating Five had organized the meeting with regulators specifically to gain special favor for Charles Keating. The impression that was given by McCain was that he was the only good senator, the only one there who was not asking any favors for the man who had transferred vast amounts of wealth into McCain's control. To some observers, McCain bent the truth.

McCain himself admitted that he lied once. Months after the South Carolina primary, he claimed that he had been lying about his support of the Confederate flag. And as mentioned before, he lied about knowing that his ancestors owned no slaves when he knew no such information.

The point is this: the truth may be a moving target with John McCain.

And so we come to McCain's February 17 "gook" comments. John McCain said, in reference to his "gook" comments, "I'm referring to our prison guards." Does McCain mean that on February 17 he was calling only his prison guards "gooks"? Or is McCain claming that he has, in his life, referred only to his prison guards as "gooks"?

Although McCain, his spokesmen, and his reporters are not clear about this, they certainly *imply* that McCain has only *ever* used the word "gook" in reference to his prison guards.

Can we trust McCain on this issue? Or is he lying again?

Consider this. McCain had not provided such caveats in the past. McCain's habit, as far as we can tell, was to casually refer to Vietnamese people as "gooks." He never said to reporters, "When I say 'gooks,' I only mean my prison guards."

But now that he was drawing heat, he decided that the only real "gooks" were his "prison guards." Sounds like a curvature of the truth.

In earlier chapters, I've documented instances in which McCain referred to Vietnamese who were not his prison guards as "gooks." He writes, for instance, that he called *the North Vietnamese in general* "gooks." In the account, he also refers to *individuals who were not prison guards* as "gooks."

Because of the media's friendship with John McCain, we will never know exactly who John McCain called "gook," from the time he returned from Vietnam in 1973 to February 17, 2000, when the media began paying closer attention.

The truth, however, is clear. John McCain referred to Vietnamese people in general as "gooks." It is safe to say that John McCain used the word "gook" just like everyone else uses the word "gook" — to insult people by *dehumanizing their race*. He dehumanized the North Vietnamese and the South Vietnamese. He insulted Asians. And he spat on his own people — Americans of Asian descent and, hence, all Americans.

QUESTIONING THE EXCUSE

Does it matter who John McCain called "gook"? Is it not racist, no matter who the racial slur is applied to?

Only Asian American writers have cared enough to examine this point. "Gook" refers to all Vietnamese, and in fact, all Asians. If you look at the history of the word, it refers to all people of color. When one is calling another person a "gook," even if one is "referring to our prison guards," one has already referred to the Vietnamese.

"If anybody doesn't believe that these interrogators and these prison guards who tortured me and my friends were not cruel and sadistic people that deserve the appellation 'gook,'" McCain said. So, John McCain prefers to refer to someone's *Asian race* in order to insult them for being sadistic and evil. What kind of association is that? McCain could have used the word "devils," or "sadists," or "evil men," but he chose to use a word that specifies their race.

Does John McCain want us to associate the sadistic nature of the guards with Asian females and males? Or does John McCain himself believe that Asians are naturally sadistic?

McCain chose to use a word that is a purely racist term. It is also the most hurtful term he could have used. McCain's specific word choice reveals his purpose in using it.

WHAT IF HE'D SAID "NIGGERS"?

John McCain claimed in his *U.S. News & World Report* POW account that many of his prison's guards were gay:

> Some guards would just come in and do their job. When they were told to beat you they would come in and do it. Some seemed to get a big bang out of it. A lot of them were homosexual, although never toward us. Some —who were pretty damned sadistic, seemed to get a big thrill out of the beatings.

Would it be okay then for John McCain to say to the mass media that he was kept in prison by "sadistic gook faggots"?

What if McCain's prison guards and captors were of the black race? Would we still be seriously considering McCain as a presidential candidate if for months he had talked of the sadistic "niggers"?

What would have happened if McCain had said, "I hated the niggers. I will continue to hate the niggers as long as I live."?

If McCain had used the word "nigger" a single time in his political career, he would have been automatically disqualified for the presidency. And rightly disqualified.

If John McCain had called a single person a "kike," he would have been automatically disqualified for the presidency. If McCain had referred to Panamanian strongman Manuel Noreiga or Cuban dictator Fidel Castro as a "spic," he would have lost any chance to make it to the White House.

The only reason — literally the *only* reason — that we still consider John McCain a serious candidate for president is that he used an anti-*Asian* slur.

If you, dear reader, are still considering voting for John McCain, you might question yourself. If John McCain had for years been calling people, *any people*, "niggers," "spics," "kikes," "crackers," "sand niggers," "faggots," "cunts," "bitches," or "ho's," would you still be considering casting your vote for him?

Ask yourself this: If any *other* candidate had used racial epithets against human beings, would you still consider voting for that candidate?

The wily John McCain chose the perfect dehumanizing comment. He was the only candidate who could get away with consistently using racial epithets, and Asians and Asian Americans were the only group that Americans were okay with allowing a candidate to "spit" on. And the year 2000 was probably the last election year in which the media and the public would have *not* disqualified McCain for the presidency in response to his racist remarks.

John McCain is a very clever or a very lucky man.

Chapter 08
Spit and Dignity

Letter to the Editor:

The more I see and hear about Sen. John McCain, the more I can guarantee a vote for "the other guy." I'm sorry McCain was held as a prisoner of war. Having served in the Army for five years, he has my respect for having survived. I also understand his anger and hate for his captors. But his free use of the word "gook" in describing his captors instead of calling them "my captors," sends up a red flag for me. This racist term is evidence of his extreme hate for his captors.

If he is elected to the presidency and a conflict comes up with an Asian nation, I'm worried he would be more apt to shoot first and talk it over after.

Kurt Bennett, League City
Published in *The Houston Chronicle*, February 24, 2000

Letter to the Editor:

Please explain how it is that Sen. John McCain can say, "I hated the gooks and will continue to hate them as long as I live," and be allowed to explain it away by referring to his storied tribulations as a POW ["Racial Issues Dog GOP Foes," news story, Feb. 18]. The term "gook" is as purely racist as the "N-word." No candidate could credibly defend his use of that epithet by saying, "I didn't mean all black people, just the ones I don't like." Why is Mr. McCain being given a pass for doing exactly the same thing?

> Andrew S. Wolfe
> Published in the *Washington Post*, Feb. 24, 2000

To the Editor:

When questioned about his use of the racially derogatory term "gook" to refer to his Vietnamese captors, Senator John McCain did so again and said, "You can quote me" (news article, Feb. 18). This epithet has widely understood connotations that go far beyond Vietnam. As people of Asian and Pacific Islander descent know from painful experience, this slur is hurled at them with no regard to national origin or whether a person had the remotest connection to the Vietnam War.

The lack of media and public reaction to Mr. McCain's statements and the failure to recognize this as an issue bearing on his fitness for the presidency is stunning.

> Christopher Ho
> San Francisco, Feb. 19, 2000
> Published in *The New York Times*, Feb. 25, 2000

Because of John McCain's almost histrionic response to a simple query — that he hated "the gooks" and would hate them until death — news of McCain's words spread like wildfire throughout the world.

The common people were disturbed. A McCain presidency could be a farce, a catastrophe.

The common folk were far more disturbed than their leaders were. It seemed that the greater the political power one had, the less one cared what outrageous words came out of a fellow leader. John McCain's Republican opponent could have had a field day with McCain's racial stands. But when asked on the eve of the South Carolina primary about McCain's "gook" comments, George W. Bush simply replied, "I wouldn't use the word."

Asian American leaders should have unleashed all of their righteous indignation at this point. But they did not. Their comments were relatively mild. Perhaps Asian American leaders felt it was outside of their job duties to comment on a presidential candidate. Perhaps the Asian American leaders did not want to anger powerful elected officials. Whatever the case, the leaders did not seem to mirror in their response the frustration, concern, anxiety and extreme disappointment among common Asian Americans.

McCain stood by his words and he stood by the Confederate flag. He had no reason to back off. He had won the New Hampshire primary, and his Straight Talk Express had charmed the media. McCain was poised to take South Carolina by storm.

SOUTH CAROLINA

None of the pundits, reporters, or advisers believed that McCain's repeated "gook" comments would hurt his chances of winning the South Carolina primary. The assumption was that because few Asian Americans lived in South Carolina, few South Carolinians would care about this issue.

On February 19, McCain soundly lost the South Carolina primary to George W. Bush. Had there been a backlash against McCain's controversial stand on the Confederate flag? Any black backlash was muted by the continued lack of voting stations in predominantly black rural areas of the state. Neither Republican candidate seemed concerned about this issue of African American voting rights.

Perhaps it was George Bush's attack ads that did McCain in. Among Bush's tactics during the South Carolina primary was a race–baiting "whisper" campaign that John McCain had fathered an illegitimate black child. Of course, this offered many reasons for right–wing Republicans to vote against McCain: many of them disliked blacks, disliked childbirth out of wedlock, and hated sex between the races. John McCain criticized Bush's tactics, saying, "I will not take the low road to the highest office in this land. I want the presidency in the best way, not the worst way."

John McCain lost largely because he *only split* the veterans vote. About one quarter of all primary voters were veterans. McCain, a Vietnam War hero, should have won the veterans vote handily. Why didn't he? Veterans are not stupid. As evidenced by the letter to the editor of the *Houston Chronicle*, perhaps veterans saw in McCain a man who has not withdrawn from the Vietnam War. The vast majority of Vietnam veterans do not say the "gook" slur in public. And few would want to be quoted in the mass media using that word. They know that it is offensive and racist. Could it be that some veterans in the conservative state of South Carolina were disturbed by McCain's racial slurs?

It seems that John McCain's white supremacist partner in South Carolina — Richard Quinn — had convinced McCain that the majority of South Carolinians were like him: secretly resentful of MLK Day, wanting to throw racial epithets in the face of the American public, and proud of a long–gone Dixieland.

George Bush proved to be a much cleverer campaigner. Bush declared that the Confederate flag issue was a states' rights issue; by using the "states' rights" phrase, Bush signaled to those who supported the Southern Cross that he was using the Confederacy's anti–U.S. language without alienating those who saw themselves as part of a "new South" where racism was not a part of official state government. McCain, on the other hand, was a little too honest. He accurately portrayed the flag issue as a clear choice between embracing the South's racist "heritage" and embracing a clean break from that past. When McCain unabashedly embraced that old, nasty "heritage," he revealed too much of himself.

A REVOLUTION OF SPIT

Acts of racism have acted as the chief catalysts for change in the political attitudes of Asian America. In some ways, then, Asian Americans should thank John McCain for bringing about a watershed event in Asian American history.

John McCain knew that as a Senator in Arizona, he should easily beat George W. in California. But suddenly there was a problem. Publicity about McCain's "gook" comments had intensified. After all, Asian Americans comprised a major swing vote in California, making up well over 10% of the population, and numbering more than the black population.

"Gook" is a much-hated racial epithet in Asian America. The word is associated with racially-motivated hate crimes. Asian Americans regularly deal with being called "gook" or "jap" or "chink" or "flip" or "VC" or "Charlie" or "Commie." The words are associated with being intimidated, screamed at, having one's home or place of worship vandalized, being spat on, having trash thrown on oneself, being robbed, having one's place of business set on fire, and being assaulted.

The 1980s and 1990s were the heyday for racist attacks against Asian Americans. In the year 2000, Asian Americans were still reeling from the famous baseball bat murder of Vincent Chin by white men in Detroit (his killers were sentenced to probation); various hate murders in North Carolina, Florida, Louisiana, Boston, and other places; and hate murders that seemed related to the murderers' fantasies about the Vietnam War.

Patrick Purdy played out his Vietnam War fantasy by killing five Southeast Asian children and wounding 30 at a Stockton, California playground. Like Rambo, he shot a machine gun.

There was the Vietnamese boy — Hung Truong — who was kicked to death by white supremacist skinheads in Houston; he pled for his life and promised he would return to Vietnam.

John McCain had to do something about his image among Asian Americans in California. He knew he had support among Vietnamese refugees in California. Traditionally, the Vietnamese refugees of the state supported the Republican Party for its extreme opposition to the Vietnamese Communist Party. Most of them fought actively against the Communist government during the war and/or were kicked out of that nation for being the "wrong" class or ethnic group or political orientation.

Many Vietnamese Americans admired John McCain for his war service. Others considered him a traitor for working for political and economic reconciliation with the Communist government in Vietnam. It's unclear what Vietnamese Americans thought of McCain's idea that the Vietnam War could have been won by dropping millions of more tons of bombs, napalm, and Agent Orange on the Vietnamese; frankly, their opinion may have hinged on who those bombs were dropped on.

Although there was a diversity of opinion among the Vietnamese immigrants and refugees, it was sometimes ill-advised to express dissent, or even to fly the current (Communist) Vietnamese flag rather than the Republic of Vietnam flag that Vietnamese Americans generally prefer.

Flags are important symbols. While some Vietnamese American "Communist sympathizers" have been assassinated in California, Texas, and elsewhere, the most famous clash within the Vietnamese American community was the case of Truong Van Tran, a Vietnamese American video store owner in Little Saigon (Westminster, California). In 1999, he posted in his store the flag of Communist Vietnam along with a picture of an old Vietnamese man, which was widely considered a stand-in for Ho Chi Minh. Vietnamese Americans protested for months in several cities around the nation until the video store was permanently shut down. Community leader Kiem Do commented on the flag controversy: "Many of my friends spent 13 to 15 years in prison camps," Do said. "After 1975, millions fled and became boat people. We lost 300,000 at sea. For those people to have Ho Chi Minh's picture displayed, it's like someone waving a Confederate flag in a black neighborhood." Do said that the store owner was simply trying to provoke his own community. Truong Van Tran was, during the controversy, arrested for making pirate copies of Asian soap operas.

Upon the closing of the shop, protestors shifted their focus on city councilman Tony Lam, who was the first Vietnamese American elected to public office in the United States. Although he had expressed support for the store protests, he had not showed up at any of the protests, so he was seen as soft on Communists.

Also fresh in the minds of Asian Americans and Vietnamese Americans in Orange County were two hate murders. In 1996, Thien Minh Ly was killed at a Tustin high school tennis court; the Vietnamese American was called a "Jap" by the murderer. In 1993, Loc Minh Truong was killed by white teenagers at nearby Laguna Beach; they called him a "faggot," and likely, other epithets. And most recently, a student of UC-Irvine in Orange County had sent life-threatening emails to 59 Asian students. Wrote the racist to the Asian students: "I hate Asians, including you. I will hunt all of you down and kill you. I personally will make it my life career to find and kill every one of you personally."

In walks John McCain. He planned a rally in Little Saigon for March 1, 2000, hoping to encourage the 120,000 Vietnamese Americans in Little Saigon to vote for him in the March 7 primaries. While many Vietnamese continued to support McCain as an anti-Communist warrior, cracks had appeared in his armor. Responding to McCain's "gook" comments, Councilman Tony Lam said, "That is bad. He doesn't know what's right from wrong. That's the word GIs used against the Viet Cong, but that's been used (in America) as a racial term against the Vietnamese."

Even George W. Bush gained the moral high ground on McCain. "He has to answer for using that word," said Bush in Los Angeles. "That's a word I'm never gonna use."

Campaigning in Seattle, McCain demonstrated that he still did not understand what the problem is with calling a human being a "gook." According to the *Washington Post*, just three days after his loss in South Carolina, McCain said that Asian Americans should not be offended, as his North Vietnamese captors' "behavior was indescribably unconscionable." Even though it had been said over and over again by Asian American leaders, it did not seem to matter to McCain that words like "gook" and "nigger" are inherently racist. He seemed to argue that it was okay to be racist when speaking of bad people. For instance, if an African American murderer were sitting in the electric chair, according to McCain, Americans shouldn't fret if a politician says, "I'm glad we're frying that nigger."

On February 23, Mai Van On, then 82 years old, said that he wanted John McCain to apologize for McCain's "gook" comments. Mai Van On was the North Vietnamese soldier who rescued John McCain. According to Mai Van On, he dragged the unconscious McCain from the lake and prevented an angry mob of Vietnamese civilians (apparently angry at the U.S. dropping bombs on them) from killing him. "I cannot believe that John McCain would say such things," On said in response to McCain's slurs. "I am sure it was just a mistake, but if he said these words I think he should apologize."

Furthermore, McCain's statement that he "hated the gooks" and would always hate "the gooks" threatened the derailing of a trade pact between the United States and Vietnam. The trade pact would have been the crowning jewel of years of work on the part of John McCain, John Kerry, and Bill Clinton to reconcile relations between the two nations. The trade pact meant billions of dollars in profits for both American corporations and Communist Party members of the Vietnamese government. It would be less profitable, after all, for Nike Corporation to move their factories to Vietnam without lower U.S. tariffs on Vietnam–made shoes.

Responding to McCain's "gook" comments, Vietnam's Foreign Ministry spokeswoman Phan Thuy Thanh said that "The fact Mr. John McCain uses such words and makes such statements that lack goodwill hurt Vietnamese." She also said, "This statement is not worthy of a U.S. senator, especially one running for the U.S. Presidency."

Luckily for McCain, Bill Archer, among other U.S. officials, was already in Vietnam to further negotiate the trade deal. It is unclear what would have happened if McCain had continued to make "gook" comments. Perhaps the trade deal would have been nixed to protect the images of both governments.

As the California primary drew near, McCain knew what he had to do. On February 24, he apologized by saying these words at a news conference:

"I was asked a question about these individuals who beat and tortured my friends. And yes, usually the words I used describing them are not printable nor should be carried over family (TV) stations," he said.

"The fact is if I offended anyone I apologize for it. But I do not apologize for the fact that my description of these people (as) bad, mean and evil people who were responsible for the deaths of my friends and I will hold a very strong opinion about them," McCain said.

His apology included the often lampooned "if I offended anyone, I apologize" phrase which is considered, even by sports fans (who hear these types of apologies often), the hallmark of an insincere apology. A good apology usually is addressed to a specific party, indicates what wrong the apologizer committed, and how it hurt the offended party.

McCain, though, was able to turn his conditional apology into a threat of violence. According to Reuters, "[McCain] said if he ever ran into one of his captors again he might have 'a little trouble controlling myself because of what they did, not to me, but to my friends who are no longer with us.' The remark drew applause from McCain supporters who watched the news conference."

As McCain continued to maneuver his way into a more non-racist image in California, people all over the nation continued to discuss McCain's "gook" comments and why the media did not cover it for months. Anger and concern about a McCain presidency was a hot topic, especially among Asian Americans. But the head of the California Republican Party, Jon Fleischman, spun the racism story another way. He said *the media* created the issue, not John McCain himself. In late February, Fleischman stated "People call here all day long, and nobody's calling about that. My definition of a media-generated story is that people on the street aren't talking about it. The only people talking about it are the reporters." Of course, Fleishman's contention was untrue. Many people were talking about McCain's racial slurs, but they weren't interested, apparently, in talking to him about it.

Simultaneous to this spin, McCain tried a different tactic in regards to Asians and Asian Americans. McCain's website featured a fortune cookie out of which came a fortune for the Democratic Party: "You will receive a donation from the Chinese Army."

McCain also tried to distract from his own racism by attacking George Bush for speaking at Bob Jones University in South Carolina, a school that does not allow inter-racial dating and whose founder has expressed views considered anti-Catholic. "That's racism," said McCain of Bush's choice of venue, "That's out-and-out racism." After the campaign, McCain would say that he himself was open to speaking at Bob Jones University.

At some point in late February, McCain's campaign released a more formal, more acceptable apology: "I will continue to condemn those who unfairly mistreated us. But out of respect to a great number of people whom I hold in very high regard, I will no longer use the term that has caused such discomfort. I deeply regret any pain I may have caused by my choice of words. I apologize and renounce all language that is bigoted and offensive, which is contrary to all that I represent and believe."

McCain and his writers wrote a well-crafted statement. It resembles, ironically, the carefully crafted statement he would recite in South Carolina concerning the Confederate flag. In that statement, he wanted to hint that he was "in" with the white supremacist stands taken by his campaign manager Richard Quinn while not coming out and saying it directly. Here he hoped to prove that he was sincerely contrite without admitting that he had been racist or that he himself was a racist.

Despite McCain's apologies, all was not well. The roiling emotions that John McCain had stirred up within Asian America could not and would not be calmed by a press conference.

People on the ground decided that they could not simply forget that McCain had called Asians "gooks." Just because an apology had been written and released does not mean it was sincere, some felt. Just because the media was satisfied, did not mean that the grass-roots felt anything but continued disgust. After all, beneath the apologizing McCain there seemed to be a hateful racist McCain.

According to the local mainstream media, McCain's March 1 rally in Little Saigon was a rousing success fit for a war hero. "A Hero's Welcome for McCain in Little Saigon," was the headline in the *Los Angeles Times*.

"McCain's Visit Stirs Admiration," headlined *The Orange County Register*. On stage, McCain introduced his fellow war heroes: South Vietnamese soldiers and citizens who had spent over a decade in Communist Vietnamese prisons. He announced their names and the amount of time they had spent in Communist prisons.

The Washington Post quoted a local Vietnamese. "He fought for us, he knows my people, so we must support him now," said Hung Nguyen, 58, a contractor who fled Vietnam by boat in 1975. "He knows the Communists very well from his years in prison, and he knows how to help us."

In general, the crowd supported McCain. It was a McCain rally after all, as well as a rally for the anti–Communist efforts of the local Vietnamese during the War. Interestingly, though, the short, war–oriented speech prompted one Vietnamese local to say that he was disappointed, as he wanted to hear more about education and other issues. After all, he explained to *the Washington Post*, the war was long ago.

Many in the crowd likely cheered McCain not knowing the full story. When one young woman heard at the rally that McCain had been using the g–word, she asked her mother, "Did he really call us 'gooks'?" The mother, holding an American flag and a Vietnamese flag hushed her up with a "Shhhhh."

Perhaps McCain would have extended his "rambling, patronizing 20–minute speech," as the *Orange County Weekly* called it, had there not been unrest astir among the crowd. A UC–Irvine student, in protest of McCain's racist epithet usage, brought with him to the rally a group of Asian American students, likely from local colleges and high schools. The student's name was Bao Nguyen. In the only published, detailed account of the incident, R. Scott Moxley and Vu Nguyen described what happened in an *Orange County Weekly* article entitled, "Quiet Riot":

> To dramatize his point at the rally, [Bao] Nguyen and his fellow student protestors wore last–minute handmade T–shirts that read, "American Gook." Standing before a startled crowd of mostly older Vietnamese–Americans, Nguyen yelled into his bullhorn, "Are you a gook?"

"No," the students shouted back. This identical exchange was repeated several times.

What happened next is one of those odd, unexpected but ugly moments that American politics seems to produce. The peaceful protestors suddenly found them selves surrounded and under physical attack—by older Vietnamese-Americans. They were repeatedly kicked, shoved and spit on. Dozens of times, the attackers screamed, "Communists!" and, "Go back to Hanoi!" Two female protesters were kicked in their stomachs and fell to the pavement. Nguyen and fellow UCI student Kwok Louie pleaded for calm. They were greeted with shouts of "Down with Communists!" One man issued a direct threat of violence. Later, one of the aggressors claimed that "If you're anti-McCain, you're a communist." Perhaps symbolic of the crowd's views, one man held a poster that read, "Gook = Communist Only."

Within minutes, the protesters—no thanks to the uninterested Westminster police officers looking on—had been pushed back about 40 feet into oncoming traffic on Bolsa Avenue. Remarkably, Nguyen—though visibly shaken, his face splattered with spit—stood dignified beyond his years. He renewed his call for calm, acceding to the crowd's demand to take his "American Gook" T-shirt off.

"Dear people, we love our country like you do. We hate communism like you do," he said in perfect Vietnamese. "But we don't agree with the word 'gook.' It's wrong. It's hurtful. People need to be educated about that."

When the cops eventually snapped out of their haze, they began using their batons to push the student protestors back toward the hostile crowd.

"Get back on the sidewalk," they ordered. More than 40 minutes after the shoving began and with reporters swooping in for interviews, tensions finally broke.

With his shirt torn, and fresh spit wiped off his face, reporters took pictures of Bao Nguyen. And they asked him questions. "When you say that word," Nguyen explained, "it breeds hate, no matter what he meant. It's insensitive to every Asian. To Americans, that gook he's talking about and me, we both look alike."

As the *Washington Post* reported, an elderly woman then interrupted him. "Communists!" she shouted. "He means communists."

"The older generation just doesn't understand," Nguyen said. Nguyen explained to the *OC Weekly*: "I didn't want to upset those people; I'm part of them. That's my community. I respect their experiences. But when things like this happen, it's discouraging."

Indeed, it was Nguyen's community. He was a typical second-generation Vietnamese American. His parents fled Saigon in 1980, and he was the sixth of seven children, growing up in Garden Grove in Orange County. He had volunteered to help flood victims in Vietnam and represented UC-Irvine on the Irvine City Council.

What happened on March 1, 2000 represented a civil conflict raging throughout Asian America.

Asian immigrants came to America wishing simply for a place where they could live free of war and strife. A place where they could work hard and prosper like nowhere else in the world. The granting of a green card, an H-1B visa, or citizenship were among their major life events. It meant they had made it.

Asian Americans born in the United States were never satisfied with just their automatic citizenship. Rather than being born in the country of their ancestors and being treated with respect and living with dignity, many Asian Americans born in this nation grew up being told, day after day, through words, images, looks, body language, mass media, and sheer intuition, that they were considered by the majority of this nation somehow, in some or many ways, inferior, undesirable, unusual, exotic, an object, a second or third class citizen, a gook.

What happened on March 1, 2000 was the younger generation of Asian America rising up to their parents and declaring, "You may have fought against Communists, Fascists, right-wing regimes, left-wing regimes, war, famine, repression, colonialism, apartheid, and all sorts of hell. And you may have felt like you made it when you got here to the United States. And you may have imagined that life for us, your children, should be perfect. But we've got a fight of our own. We fight for our dignity. And yes, that matters. We've been fighting for it since we were born. And we don't want to wait another day to achieve equality in every way in our nation. We refuse to be guests, prisoners, displays, renters, sojourners, temporary help or anything but the owners of our home, America!"

The spit that covered Bao Nguyen and the other Asian American students on March 1, 2000 represented the repudiation by the older generation of the younger generation. It was almost as if the older generation believed the younger generation did not appreciate all the tremendous blood, sweat, tears, soul, and heart that the older generation had left in the soil of the earth in establishing their lives here in the United States. It was as if the older generation was making one last, desperate attempt to tell the younger ones, "Don't make waves. Be satisfied with what you have got, what we have gotten for you. We don't have a beef with the white man. Appreciate your life in America."

Before March 1, 2000, Asian Americans fought in the courts for the rights of people who had been victims of racial violence. They fought against racial discrimination. They fought for their right not be deported or detained in internment camps. They fought against institutionalized racism. But as seen by the reluctance, shyness, and hesitance of Asian American leaders during McCain's "gook" remarks, the older generation did not share the younger generation's desire to hold sway over not only the politics and the economics but also the culture, the media, and the social interactions of this, our nation. In every aspect of life, every last one of them, we want to live in dignity, the young ones shouted, and it was a shout, a call, an exhortation heard quietly over the internet and newspaper clippings and CNN throughout the nation. Perhaps not so many Asian Americans knew about the events of March 1, 2000 as they knew about the murder of Vincent Chin or the election of Gary Locke as governor of Washington State. But somehow, the story of young Asian Americans running a gauntlet of spit and kicks from those whose judgment they feared most (the older generations of their community) in order to demand something that has been rarely demanded — our right to live in dignity, without senators smearing us — this story sank like fresh rainwater into the thirsty soil of the collective subconscious of Asian America.

And from that day forward, Asian America was more apt to fight for everything they had coming to them — our rights, our freedom, our dignity. It was clearer than ever before:

We demand it all.

Chapter 09
Give Wars a Chance

After the tumultuous March 1 rally, John McCain returned to the sanctuary of his Straight Talk Express and assessed the event for himself and for the media: "There were a couple of protestors and a couple of thousand enthusiastic loving supporters," he said. "I think it's the diversity of America." Had he nothing to say about his role in stirring up the ruckus within the Vietnamese and Asian American communities?

On to more urgent matters: starting new wars. The next day, March 2, John McCain announced that if he were elected president, he would unilaterally withdraw the U.S. from the Anti–Ballistic Missile Treaty with Russia.

To quote his press release: "Russia must be made to understand that we will not allow our people to be vulnerable to ballistic missile attack from North Korea, Iraq, or any other nation that may seek to threaten our nation," wrote McCain. Withdrawal from the treaty allows Russia to develop anti–ballistic missile technology, and gives Russia an excuse to mistrust the United States and ignore our diplomacy.

McCain was cleverly shifting attention away from Russia, a nation we would never dare start a war with, and towards more reasonable war partners, such as North Korea and Iraq.

At the time, Russia was fighting the Second Chechen War without any regard for human life. While both sides in the war argued that the other was wrong and evil, Russia showed little restraint in killing between 25,000 and 50,000 Chechen civilians in order to re-incorporate Chechnya into the Russian state. Most of those dead civilians, though, were Muslim. Perhaps that is why McCain disregarded that slaughter and concentrated on invading another Muslim nation: Iraq.

Not only did McCain give Russia the green light for whatever nastiness they wished to unleash on the Chechens, he also signaled that Russia could and should build an anti-ballistic missile system themselves. In that case, Russia would become the nuclear superpower of the world, prompting a renewed arms race between Western democracies and the Putin government. It did not matter. What mattered was the opportunity to start wars, apparently, against nations who possessed *no* nuclear weapons (Iraq, Libya). And perhaps what mattered even more was the tremendous military contracts required to develop a U.S. anti-ballistic missile system.

John McCain was preparing the United States for an invasion of Iraq as early as 1999, years before George Bush got around to invading Iraq. McCain's top foreign policy adviser worked towards an Iraq invasion as early as 1998.

McCain's foreign policy was based on "rogue state rollback." It's not clear when McCain came up with the catchphrase, but it's inconceivable that he had not worked on the concept for years. He explained "rogue state rollback" to the American people on February 15, 2000 during a debate moderated by Larry King. The candidates were asked by King, "What area of American international policy would you change *immediately* as president?" What follows is the exchange between McCain and King:

McCain: China is obviously a place where this — one of the signal failures of this administration. Although there are certainly many failures throughout the world.

But I would also look very — revise our policies concerning these rogue states: Iraq, Libya, North Korea — those countries that continue to try to acquire weapons of mass destruction and the means to deliver them. As long...

King: And you'd do what?

McCain: I'd institute a policy that I call "rogue state roll-back." I would arm, train, equip, both from without and from within, forces that would eventually overthrow the governments and install free and democratically elected governments.

As long as Saddam Hussein is in power, I am convinced that he will pose a threat to our security. "The New York Times" reported just a few days ago that administration officials worry that Saddam Hussein continues to develop weapons of mass destruction.

Congress passed a law a couple of years ago, called the Iraqi Liberation Act; the administration has done nothing. We should help them with arms, training, equipment, radio and a broad variety of ways. Until those governments are overthrown, they will pose a threat to U.S. national security.

If pressure on these rogue nations did not work, McCain said on December 7, 1999, "We must be prepared to back up these measures with American military force if the existence of such rogue states threatens America's interests and values." Long before September 11, 2001, John McCain sought to start wars in multiple nations. In a McCain presidency, rather than a

Bush presidency, the United States would have gladly launched itself into a decade-long war in Iraq, even without using September 11 as an excuse.

While most Americans remember fondly the Bill Clinton years for its lack of full-out war, McCain was frustrated by the lack of military action. Writes Dreyfuss:

> At the height of the crisis in Kosovo, McCain clamored for an invasion, bitterly criticizing the Clinton Administration for its "excessively restricted air campaign" and its decision to "refrain from using ground troops," adding: "These two mistakes were made in what almost seemed willful ignorance of every lesson we learned in Vietnam." Similarly, during the flare-up in 1994 over North Korea's nuclear program, McCain recklessly accused President Clinton of "appeasement" of Pyongyang, warning, "The time for more forceful, coercive action is long overdue." McCain demanded that the United States increase its alert status; mobilize US troops; deploy aircraft carriers, more fighters and Apache helicopters; pre-position bombers and tankers; and announce the immediate application of economic sanctions—even while recognizing the strong possibility that such actions could lead to war on the Korean peninsula. And on Iraq, he says that "the only way to prevail is to strike disproportionate to the provocation," criticizing the White House for "the extremely limited scale" of bombing raids there.

To put this all together: John McCain's *immediate* act, his first act, as president of the United States would be to start wars in nations that are run by governments that he considers "rogue." These wars would begin, most likely, as civil wars in which the United States armed "freedom fighters" to attack the government and its supporters. If this did not work, the United States would use their own forces to attack these states. After all, the fact that they were "rogue" and might attack the United States with (imagined) ballistic missiles was a "threat to American interests and ideas." The U.S. invasion of these nations would begin with bombing.

Drawing from McCain speeches, bombing seems to be his preferred type of military violence. It kills large numbers of people (especially civilians). It risks fewer American troops than a ground invasion, and therefore it is more politically expedient. According to McCain's Vietnam comments — that the bombing was not extensive enough — the limit on civilian deaths might be stretched into the ten-millions before McCain decided that bombing had failed and that American ground troops should be sent in to do the job. And reading into McCain's comment that he'd keep American troops in Iraq for a century, or as long as necessary, McCain's wars against these "rogue states" may never end.

Furthermore, McCain would have invaded Iraq and Libya immediately, even before September 11th, 2001. The 9/11 attacks gave the United States, in the eyes of the world, some minimal justification for their invasion of Afghanistan, even if our primary objective was not to capture Osama bin Laden. If McCain had launched insurrections in Iraq and Libya before 9/11, he would have caused many more millions of people to hate the United States. And those angry people are the soil in which terrorists are grown.

John McCain is at this moment the most dangerous person in the world. He has always been a far more eager hawk than George W. Bush, and how many wars would that "war president," as Bush fancies himself, launch us into if he had his druthers?

But what does McCain's hawkishness have to do with race? American presidents tend to start civil wars, initiate military coups, arm terrorist "freedom fighters," train death squads, help torturers, and bomb cities when those civilians at risk are people of color.

Racism feeds war, and war feeds racism. I have written some on McCain's racial attitudes. To show his affinity for war reveals a terrible combination. A strong racial antipathy chained to a tendency to launch bombing campaigns means that both of these attributes will only fuel the fire of the other.

McCain supported the contra guerilla group in Nicaragua. He supported them before their brutal and sadistic methods were made public, and he supported them after, too. He supported them even after the U.S. government had decided to cut off support to the terrorist "freedom fighters." McCain supported the contras so much that, according to the *Washington Post* (Feb. 9, 1988):

> Nicaraguan rebel leaders, scrambling for a survival strategy in the wake of congressional refusal last week to appropriate new aid funds, pleaded today for independent financial contributions from U.S. supporters to two private foundations based in Washington.
>
> The contra leaders said Republican presidential candidate Robert Dole recently contributed $500 to rebel coffers, and Sen. John McCain (R–Ariz.) donated $400.

The contras were well-known for their methods of raping, torturing and killing civilians, oftentimes in the most sexually sadistic and bizarre manners. The contras so habitually killed large numbers of civilians that Americas Watch called this their standard operating procedure.

The Catholic Institute for International Relations wrote in their 1987 human rights report: "The record of the contras in the field, as opposed to their official professions of democratic faith, is one of consistent and bloody abuse of human rights, of murder, torture, mutilation, rape, arson, destruction and kidnapping."

The Christian peace organization, Witness for Peace, documented that the contras had the habit of cutting off the sexual organs of both women and men, cutting off arms, gouging out eyes, pouring acid on people, raping girls, and bayoneting pregnant women. When an uncontrolled armed group receives free money from the U.S. government, they are essentially given free reign over the civilians who continue living only at their mercy.

Because Congress had cut off funding to the contras, elements within the Reagan Administration organized illegal sales of arms to Iran in order to send the money to the contras in Nicaragua. Ollie North, a man who seemed happy to "blow up Nicaragua," as he put it, was the fall guy convicted in this unconstitutional supplying of aid to both the contras and the "Islamic fascists" in Iran. McCain likes to hint at treason in others. North should have been convicted of treason, but the Reagan administration, which orchestrated the treasonous activity, was still in power. In 1989, North was convicted of accepting an illegal gratuity, aiding and abetting in the obstruction of a congressional inquiry, and destruction of documents. He never served a day in prison.

Five years later, Ollie North ran for the U.S. Senate, and John McCain endorsed him. He was one of the very few who endorsed North, a man who had supplied arms to Iranian terrorists and reprehensible guerillas by committing many of the worst constitutional crimes in American history. In 2008, McCain's campaign proudly distributed news that Ollie North had endorsed McCain for president.

Did McCain himself break the law? McCain's dealings with the contras had the air of an illegal, sick war, much like his support of the bombing of Cambodia. Here is an excerpt from a September 2, 1987 *Washington Post* story describing a "diplomatic" visit to Central America:

> McCain and Symms said they visited a contra military camp in Honduras Monday morning. The Aug. 7 peace plan, signed in Guatemala, calls for such bases to be shut down. The Honduran government has denied it has any contra camps in its territory.

McCain, a major supporter of the contras, went to visit a contra military camp that violated a peace plan. The visit likely gave the contras the message that the United States supported the contras whether or not they complied with this peace plan. Indeed, when McCain returned to the United States, he argued to the White House that the contras should be allowed to maintain their illegal military camps.

John McCain supported military aid to a Salvadoran government whose death squads killed tens of thousands of civilians in their tiny nation.

But McCain had enough political sense to join a unanimous Senate in condemning that government when it killed six prominent Jesuit priests, their housekeeper, and her daughter. But of course, the military aid to that government must continue!

In 1989, McCain voted for an amendment to the foreign aid bill that supplied aid to the military groups fighting the "never-ending civil war" (as the *Congressional Quarterly* called it) in Cambodia. The amendment said that the aid should not go to the Khmer Rouge, but since the aid was going to the Khmer Rouge's military allies, this statement had no meaning. By sending supplies to the Khmer Rouge's allies, the U.S. supported the Khmer Rouge.

In this effort, the United States cooperated with that paragon of human rights, the Communist Party of China.

The Khmer Rouge killed between one million and three million Cambodians when they ruled Cambodia between 1975 and 1978. Their insane Maoist policies resulted in one of the worst genocides in history. Sadly, the Khmer Rouge's rise to power in Cambodia was very much aided by Nixon's overthrow of Prince Sihanouk and his secret bombing of Cambodia, which John McCain praised.

Why did McCain support genocidal maniacs?

The Khmer Rouge were battling a Cambodian government that was backed by the Vietnamese Communist Party. In 1978, Vietnam invaded Cambodia, overthrew the Khmer Rouge and installed an authoritarian but non-genocidal government. Since then, the Khmer Rouge had been waging war against that government in an effort to regain power.

By voting for the 1989 amendment, McCain was putting Cambodians at risk of a second genocide. But McCain, it seems, could not let go of the Vietnam War. By supporting the anti-government rebels, which included the Khmer Rouge, McCain was able to continue fighting a war against the Vietnamese Communist Party, which was backing the Cambodian government. It did not matter how many more people died.

But what does any of this have to do with race? The Khmer Rouge were like the Nazis in Germany. Pol Pot was the Asian version of Adolph Hitler. Would John McCain have supported an alliance with Hitler in a continuing genocide of Jews?

Would John McCain have donated money to an armed group in Nicaragua if he knew that that group was cutting off the breasts and vaginas of blonde, white women rather than dark-haired, dark-skinned peasant women?

If the military junta in Myanmar ruled over English people rather than Southeast Asians, would John McCain have hired two U.S. lobbyists who had worked for that military junta? These lobbyists fought for U.S. support of that junta, which as I write, is preventing food and medicine to hundreds of thousands of Burmese victims of a devastating cyclone. They are sending rotten food to the starving, preventing medicine from reaching those dying from disease. The lobbyists were hired at the highest levels of McCain's campaign, and their presence further indicates that a McCain administration would view the lives of people of color living in foreign nations as negligible.

Chapter 10
"I broke my promise to always tell the truth."

Six days after the Little Saigon rally, John McCain lost nine of thirteen primaries in a Super Tuesday contest against George W. Bush. Unsurprisingly, he won the Vietnamese American vote in California, but his image among many Asian Americans was permanently damaged. He lost the California, New York, Ohio, and Georgia primaries. The loss of California, a state that neighbors his own, must have been particularly devastating. All of his wins were in New England.

On March 9, McCain withdrew from the presidential race and threw his support over the next eight years behind George W. Bush.

His loss to Bush devastated McCain and took him to a very dark place. He changed and re-changed many of his positions after that loss. And so began the Pandering Express of John McCain. The true John McCain in many ways withdrew from public life. The new John McCain is all about winning the presidency. He will do and say whatever is necessary.

In the months leading up to the 2008 election, a nationwide debate has emerged over what or who the real John McCain is. Some writers propose that there is no real John McCain, that he is simply the sum of his advisers and his overwhelming desire to become president.

Most of these writers focus on the maddening pace of John McCain's flip-flopping over the past several years. He's changed positions more often than the Kama Sutra.

He's against the Bush tax cut. He's for it. He's for amnesty for illegal immigrants. Then he's against it. He's against ethanol, he's for it. He's tinkered with the idea of being pro-choice, then returned to being pro-life. He supports clean government but lets the most mercenary lobbyists lead his campaign.

McCain owns more flip-flops than a beach-combing centipede. There are too many to delineate here in any detail. And it is unnecessary to do so.

When it comes to McCain's racial attitudes, McCain has made things quite clear to us, even when he is attempting to make himself out to be a non-racist.

McCain returned to South Carolina after he lost the 2000 Republican nomination. At a luncheon for mostly white Republicans in Columbia, South Carolina, John McCain claimed that he had lied when speaking about his support for the Confederate flag: "I feared that if I answered honestly, I could not win the South Carolina primary," McCain said. "So I chose to compromise my principles. I broke my promise to always tell the truth."

McCain's implication, then, was that he really was not a racist, as his policies and associates seemed to indicate. He was essentially saying that he had made a tactical error. This reminds me of the argument that some people make about Barry Goldwater.

Goldwater, they said, voted against the Civil Rights Act of 1964 and the Voting Rights Act of 1965 for political reasons — he was courting the Southern vote. That does not make him a racist, they argue.

If one is willing to prevent African Americans from attaining civil rights so that one can win Southern votes in a presidential campaign, then what does that make you? If you are willing to *systematically and institutionally* oppress people of color for your own personal gain, what does that make you? Is there a word in the English language that means "a person who has such little regard for a race of people that he is willing to punish, harm, oppress, or demean them in exchange for personal gain"?

When Kanye West criticized George Bush's treasonously weak response to Hurricane Katrina, Kanye West said that George Bush "doesn't care about black people." He did not call Bush a racist. He simply implied that Bush cares much, much more about white people than about black people. White people were people to him, and black people were something not quite people.

The same principle might be applied to Goldwater and McCain. If you are willing to exploit people of color in order to win votes toward the White House, and if we are not allowed to call you a racist (because that language is too extreme), then perhaps you are simply a "George Busher."

Richard Quinn, McCain's chief strategist in South Carolina and a founder of the white supremacist *Southern Partisan*, said in response to McCain's post–withdrawal revelation, "Everything he said was factual," Quinn said. "When he was asked 'How do you feel personally [about the Confederate battle flag]?' he held back. I think he was harsh on himself to say that was dishonest. He was just not forthcoming."

A black Republican candidate for Congress commented that "It would have been easy for him to just stay out of it, but he came back, so I have a lot of respect for him." He added, "It would have made it easier for minorities to be comfortable with this party if he had [been honest up front]."

Jake Knotts, a flag supporter and a Republican state representative, was less forgiving. "If he'd lie on the campaign trail, then he's no better than Bill Clinton," said the lawmaker. "He'd lie in Washington or in the White House." Knotts added, "I'm not only disappointed, I'm ashamed of him. I'm ashamed that he lied to the people of South Carolina in order to further his political career."

So when exactly did McCain lie? Did he lie when he campaigned for the Confederate flag? Or did he lie when he said that his support of the Confederate flag was all a lie?

McCain, in my estimation, lied about lying; if he had his druthers he would openly support the Confederate flag. Look at his record.

But let's assume that he is telling the truth about lying. He essentially admitted to a large group of mostly white Republicans, "I am willing to sell black folks out. I am willing to throw people of color under the bus for political gain."

Look at it from the perspective of a person of color. Yes, it does hurt to have a person as powerful as John McCain driving around your state in a bus called the "Straight Talk Express" announcing that you are a second-class citizen in your own state, your own nation. That is what the Confederate flag flying above the statehouse says: "We white folks are still superior to you in every way, and we still rule over you. And we have the flag flying over the statehouse to prove it."

Sadly, McCain said at the luncheon that he understands the dehumanizing effect of the Confederate flag. This means that McCain understood exactly how cruelly he was demeaning black people as he was doing it.

And what was McCain saying by apologizing for his racist/political act to a group of *white Republicans* rather than to the groups he should have apologized to — African Americans, Latinos, and Asian Americans throughout this nation? By apologizing to white Republicans rather than people of color, McCain essentially said, "My wrong was not in demeaning people of color, but rather in making a strategic error. I apologize, and next time I will do better for the Republican Party."

This apology was aimed at two entities: the Republican Party and the media. A more "pragmatic" McCain was already looking toward the 2008 election. Those among the mass media have claimed that the media itself is McCain's "base." And the apology sealed the deal with the media, who praised him for his "eloquent" speech rather than dissecting him like they did other right-wingers who have used racial epithets or touted racial segregation.

Republican Senate Majority Leader Trent Lott lost that title after it became public that he had praised Strom Thurmond on his 100th birthday, saying that Lott was proud to have voted for Thurmond's segregationist ticket in 1948 and that "if the rest of the country had followed our lead, we wouldn't have had all these problems over the years either." Previous to this, Lott had boasted privately that he had prevented his college fraternity from allowing black people into any of their fraternities, nationwide.

Republican Senator George Allen enjoyed flying the Confederate flag as a teenager, and when he was elected to Congress, he opposed the Martin Luther King holiday in 1984. In 2006, Allen was considered a hot prospect for the presidential run, but it all melted away when he referred to an Indian American working for the opposition as a "macaca."

Both Allen and Lott apologized for their comments. Allen even apologized to the party he insulted, unlike McCain. Allen was immediately voted out of office in 2006, and Lott, suffering from a public understanding of his true nature, resigned in disgrace from the Senate in 2007. In 2008, Allen made no attempt to run for president.

"Macaca," spoke George Allen.

"Gook," spoke McCain.

Chapter 11
English Only

"We have room for but one language in this country, and
that is the English language, for we intend to see that the
crucible turns our people out as Americans, of American
nationality, and not as dwellers in a polyglot boarding
house."

—President Theodore Roosevelt, 1914.

President Theodore Roosevelt, McCain's model president, believed that the
manufacturing plant that clones Americans must heat them in a "crucible"
until they speak English. Then they will be Americans.

The English Only movement seeks to eliminate non-English languages
from various forms of public and social interaction, from classrooms
to workplaces to government services. English Only activists can draw
inspiration from both Theodore Roosevelt and John McCain. Theodore
Roosevelt not only endorsed a monolingual society, he also enforced the

anti–Asian immigration laws with an iron fist. He made permanent the Chinese Exclusion acts, including the Geary Act, which required that Chinese Americans carry registration papers with them at all times or risk deportation. He cut off Japanese immigration through the "Gentlemen's Agreement." All of these measures helped to keep America white and English-speaking.

In contrast, John McCain at various times has supported an amnesty program for immigrants willing to work through it. But John McCain also backed off from his support of amnesty programs, rendering his original position meaningless. Furthermore, McCain has always put Teddy Roosevelt on a pedestal. McCain draws inspiration from Roosevelt's life and philosophy, and given the opportunity, McCain advanced the English Only cause.

The English Only movement is not aimed solely at immigrants. According to English–only advocates, citizens too must operate primarily in English! The first volley in the modern English Only movement may have been an "anti–bilingual" bill passed by Dade County Florida in 1980. The English Only movement caught fire in the Reagan years, and by 1988, states such as Arizona (McCain's state) and Florida had adapted English as their official language. But even in a conservative state like Texas, an English–only bill had no chance of passing.

Meanwhile, the use of multiple languages in government documents and communications continued to spread. This use of languages in addition to English helped non–native speakers deal with police, attain medical care, vote, handle emergencies and disasters, and commence their formal education in the United States.

After September 11, 2001, though, anti–immigration movements in the United States gained steam. Pundits railed against immigrants, especially those non–white ones. Minutemen lined the border to capture illegal immigrants. It resembled the earliest immigration wars in the United States, when citizens were paid money for apprehending Chinese people crossing the Southern border. And immigration agents took pictures of Asians in Juarez, to see if they matched with Asians later found in Texas.

Amidst the new American rage against immigrants, certain senators saw their opportunity to make English the only official language of the United States. John McCain represents Arizona, where almost 30% of the population is of Hispanic origin. He must, for the most part, not anger that community or risk losing re-election. Not to mention his presidential ambitions.

Nevertheless, because fighting for the English language sounds rather innocuous, McCain apparently believed he could support a move towards English only in government without risk to his electoral goals.

English-Only advocates had had difficulty passing any law that declared English the "official" language of the United States, so in 2006, Senator James Inhofe (Republican from Oklahoma) changed tactics and proposed an amendment to "declare English as the national language of the United States and to promote the patriotic integration of prospective US citizens." Of course, this all sounds nice, but the actual meat of the legislation is pernicious and anti-American:

> Unless otherwise authorized or provided by law, no person has a right, entitlement, or claim to have the Government of the United States or any of its officials or representatives act, communicate, perform or provide services, or provide materials in any language other than English. If exceptions are made, that does not create a legal entitlement to additional services in that language or any language other than English. If any forms are issued by the Federal Government in a language other than English (or such forms are completed in a language other than English), the English language version of the form is the sole authority for all legal purposes.

The amendment essentially eliminates the right of people to request and receive government services in any language except English. While the Constitution grants no right for Americans to demand that the government communicate in Spanish or French, the Constitution also does not state that government *must* operate in English.

The true devil is in the message that this law sends to state and local governments. Basically, it gives federal approval for these governments to eliminate their Spanish-language services. For instance, the federal government is saying that if a local government wants to eliminate Spanish interpreting services from its police operations, they can. They may even be encouraged by this legislation to do so. They may see it as their duty to "promote the patriotic integration" of American citizens and prospective American citizens.

911 operators and policemen would then say to the citizens in their districts, "I can't help you if you can't speak English." There is no need to have interpreters available at hospitals or mental institutions. Voting ballots can be in English only too; coincidentally, this is a boon for those right-wing legislators who support English as the only language of the United States.

Of course such changes would affect citizens and immigrants and illegal immigrants equally. The Polish grandmother seeking her social security check may be frustrated by the English "stonewall" she encounters at the government office.

The Spanish speaking grandpa might wish to apply for Medicare only after he learns how to deal with the rude clerks who happen to speak only English.

Children born in the United States whose parents are foreign are still U.S. citizens. Those children may struggle in schools where interpreters have disappeared. They may wish to say something important to a teacher or counselor, but they only know how to say it in Portuguese. Perhaps they are being sexually abused by their stepfather. "Too bad. Tell it to your parents," may essentially be the response.

The effects of the Inhofe Amendment may take years to be felt in some more culturally sensitive areas of the United States, but with every intensification of anti-immigrant sentiment and with every increase in the Nielsen ratings of CNN's Lou Dobbs, the Inhofe Amendment will eliminate more and more non-English services in the United States.

When Hurricane Katrina hit, tens of thousands of Vietnamese Americans and Hispanic Americans streamed into Texas from other states. Some city governments had to rely on community groups to interpret for people who spoke English with little proficiency. With the Inhofe amendment fully implemented, interpreter services may not be available even to victims of natural catastrophes. Similar sentiments were expressed in an open letter to the federal government:

> National Council of La Raza and its network of affiliates, which are deeply engaged in the process of integrating immigrants into American society, opposed the Inhofe amendment because it would make it more difficult for government agencies to communicate with people who speak other languages. This is more than symbolism; it is misguided and even dangerous legislation.
>
> Agencies such as the Centers for Disease Control and Prevention and the Federal Emergency Management Agency would face new obstacles when attempting to reach immigrant communities in the event of natural disasters, pandemics or other threats to public health and safety. Sen. Inhofe may believe that being concerned about the health and safety of all Americans — immigrant and non-immigrant alike — is a "radical, leftist" position to take, but those of us who work every day to help immigrants learn English believe his amendment is bad public policy, and should never become law.
>
> Lisa Navarrete, vice president
> National Council of La Raza
> Washington

With the support of President George W. Bush and the key support of senior Republican Senator John McCain, the Inhofe amendment became official, national law.

The Inhofe amendment is one of the most straight-up racist laws passed since the institution of the Asiatic Barred Zone in 1924. The Inhofe

Amendment is a betrayal of the basic premises of the Constitution, the Declaration of Independence, the 14th Amendment, and the 1964 Civil Rights Act. Not all people are created equal, and people should not be treated equally under the law. People who speak, read, and write English fluently have the right to better government services than those who speak it less proficiently.

Senator Harry Reid said after the law's passage, "This amendment is racist. I think it's directed basically at people who speak Spanish." While Reid was right about the amendment being racist, he was wrong about it being aimed solely at punishing Spanish-speakers. The amendment limits the ability of Asian, Latino, African, and European immigrants to integrate into American society.

Of course most Americans have no idea that when our "founding fathers" created the United States out of thirteen colonies, many, many languages were spoken in the United States, and many people simply could not understand each other without some work. And many of these immigrants to America did not learn much English. People spoke Spanish, German, French, Irish, English, Scottish, Dutch, Navajo, Iroquois, and many other languages. The founding fathers, all white men, decided that there could be an official bird and an official flag, but there will be no official language. Take a look at the Constitution.

Those who back English Only seem to believe that immigrants and people who speak English less proficiently have nothing else to do in their workday except learn English. They have no children to raise, they don't have two jobs to work, and they aren't often working the lowest-paying, most grueling jobs in America. No. They spend all day watching Spanish TV and not learning English.

Ludicrous. It takes time — years or decades — to learn to speak, read, and write English. Many American-born Americans whose only language is English have trouble speaking, reading, and writing the language. My grandmother spoke bad English. She tried to pick it up at the age of eighty, after moving to the United States. But it was difficult. Luckily, we were there to help her.

Others in this nation are not so lucky to have mobile interpreters going everywhere they go.

To punish immigrants, slow learners, and those children born here to foreign parents for the sake of national homogeneity smacks of a new American fascism. While John McCain generally courts Latino voters, his key support for English-only legislation shows Mr. McCain's true colors.

Chapter 12
The KKK, the CCC,
and John McCain

"I'm proud to offer my support to this committed conservative reformer." — John McCain officially endorsing
George Wallace, Jr.

John McCain, of course, is not the only presidential candidate who has been
considered a "racist."

Republican Barry Goldwater ran for president in 1964 against Democrat
Lyndon B. Johnson. Barry Goldwater was John McCain's mentor, friend, and
campaign manager. Goldwater's racial policies were on the far–right fringe
of the political spectrum. By voting against the Civil Rights Act of 1964 and
the Voting Rights Act of 1965, Goldwater sought to keep African Americans
in a never–ending state of segregation. One thing that Goldwater never did,
though, was spit out racial epithets in public.

While many consider Barry Goldwater a racist, George Wallace was deeply,
soulfully racist. Wallace, the governor of Alabama, ran for president in
1968 as the nominee of the fringe American Independent Party. He lost to

the pro–civil rights Democrat Lyndon B. Johnson. Historians have noted Wallace's easy and consistent use of the word "nigger" and "niggers." Like McCain, Wallace *wanted the public to know* he was using a racial slur. He used "nigger" to refer to the nation's first black senator since Reconstruction (Edward W. Brooke), and he once referred to Africans as "niggers."

On June 11, 1963, George Wallace attempted to block the registration of the first two black students at the University of Alabama by "standing before the schoolhouse door" as it is now famously known. He wished to intimidate or block the two young people from registering as students. It reminds one of the heyday of the KKK, when men with shotguns would stand before voting sites to prevent blacks from voting. Wanting to prevent any further hate-murders of African Americans, President John F. Kennedy federalized the Alabama National Guard to escort Vivian Malone and James Hood into the university administration building.

In November 1963, racist terrorists exploded a bomb outside of Vivian Malone's dormitory. The terrorists warned that the next bomb would be exploded in Vivian Malone's dormitory room. Just two months earlier, four African American girls were killed when the KKK exploded a bomb at a black church in nearby Birmingham, Alabama. On November 18, just four days before the assassination of President Kennedy, university vice–president Jeff Bennett took a trip to see Governor Wallace. James Hood had already left the university, but Vivian Malone refused to give up her college education even though she was now in danger of being killed. George Wallace asked Vice–President Bennett how long it would take "to get the nigger bitch out of the dormitory?"

George Wallace died in 1998, but his son, George Wallace, Jr., continued the family work in politics. Republican George, Jr. was elected twice as Alabama State Treasurer and then won election on the Public Service Commission. He wished to walk squarely in his father's footsteps by slinking his way towards his father's old haunt — the governor's mansion. In 2005, George Wallace, Jr. took on the tremendous challenge of running as a Republican for the office of Lieutenant Governor. Since the re–establishment of the Lieutenant Governor's office in 1903, only one out of 25 lieutenant governors had been a Republican.

But before Wallace could even think about running against the Democrat, he had to win the Republican primary. That would prove difficult, as there were three other Republican candidates running for the office. What made it an even greater long shot was Wallace's association with an outspoken white supremacist group.

But George Wallace had a secret weapon.

The most prominent Republican legislator in the nation would fly to Alabama to make speeches on behalf of George Wallace, Jr. It was not exactly clear why a presidential hopeful would be so interested in a relatively obscure primary race. It was not exactly clear why a presidential hopeful would fly to Alabama to endorse a man who had just spoken at the national convention of a white supremacist organization. It's not exactly clear but if one thinks about it, it is obvious.

Wallace's Republican white knight was John McCain.

> We believe that the United States derives from and is an integral part of European civilization and the European people and that the American people and government should remain European in their composition and character. We also oppose all efforts to mix the races of mankind...

So begins the mission statement of the Council of Conservative Citizens (CCC). Although the mission statement speaks of "European people," the CCC make it clear in their other writings that they mean the "white people" of European descent, and not any black Europeans or Europeans of Asian descent. And though the CCC has a relatively benign name, its name obviously parallels the better-known KKK. The proof is in the membership, though, as the CCC has attracted many former and current KKK leaders. The CCC, like the KKK, actively denigrates African Americans and provokes white rage against people of color.

On a single day (April 17, 2007, the first time I viewed their website), the CCC posted the following headlines: "Barack Hussein Obama's Anti-White Speech," "Global White Population Falling Fast," and "Another young white girl is a victim of a racially motivated group assault."

[Trivial note: the shady organizations associated with McCain tend to spell badly. The CCC featured a headline concerning "ganster rap" and the INC featured an entire page dedicated to "Iraqi libration."]

The foremost expert on, and opposition to, hate groups in the United States is the Southern Poverty Law Center (SPLC). The SPLC has documented the best information about the CCC, and my research draws from their documents, available on their website.

The CCC has referred to blacks as "a retrograde species of humanity."

Although the CCC is one of the more powerful white supremacy groups in the nation, it claims only 15,000 dues-paying members. The CCC publishes a newsletter called *Citizens Informer*, to which 20,000 Americans subscribe. The newsletter publishes racially provocative works. Stated one of its columnists: "Western civilization with all its might and glory would never have achieved its greatness without the directing hand of God and the creative genius of the white race."

CCC Columnist Robert Patterson continued, "Any effort to destroy the race by a mixture of black blood is an effort to destroy Western civilization itself... "

"Let us pray that our citizens will awaken and vote themselves out of this dilemma," Patterson wrote in another essay, "There is still time. The Civil Rights Act of 1964 and the Voting Rights Act of 1965 should be repealed!" He seemed to echo the sentiments of George Wallace and Barry Goldwater.

More writings from *The Informer*: "The whites were the creators of civilization, the yellows its sustainers and copyists, the blacks its destroyers... "

"The genocide being carried out against white people hasn't come with marching armies; instead, it has come with propaganda that is calculated to brainwash whites into happily and willingly jumping into the New–Melting Pot, and to their destruction…"

One website article claimed that Abraham Lincoln was gay, ugly, and psychotic.

An FBI informant named Vince Reed stated that the CCC's leader, Gordon Lee Baum, tried to recruit Reed. According to Reed, Baum said to him, "Vince, the Jews are going to fall from the inside, not from the outside, and the niggers will be a puppet on a string for us."

According to Reed, the CCC chief said, "The power is not out there in the gun, it is inside Congress. You can battle for the rest of your life with guns and explosives, and you aren't going anywhere. We've got to do it from the inside."

This strategy of planting white supremacist, racist seeds in the state and federal legislatures has worked. Among its measly 5,000 membership in the South, the CCC boasts 34 *state legislators*. State legislators, then, were *thousands of times more likely* to join the racist organization than ordinary citizens. While outwardly racist leaders like former KKK Grand Dragon David Duke have shown up at CCC conventions, the list of "mainstream" elected officials of the CCC remained secret.

What the CCC needed more than anything was an elected official to publicly legitimize the CCC. But who would dare "come out" as an all-out white supremacist?

George Wallace, Jr. waited until the last year of his father's life before he began his public support for the CCC. Wallace gave three speeches to the CCC between 1998 and 1999. In June 2005, George Wallace, Jr. kicked off the national convention of the CCC, making a speech to more than 100 CCC delegates from around the nation. Among them were the top hate leaders in the nation:

> Don Black, former Alabama grand dragon of the Knights
> of the Ku Klux Klan and proprietor of Stormfront.org, the
> most influential hate site on the internet; Jamie Kelso,
> right–hand man and Louisiana roommate of former Klan

leader David Duke; Jared Taylor, editor of the neo-eu-genicist *American Renaissance* magazine; Ed Fields, an aging white supremacist leader from Georgia; Alabama CCC leader Leonard "Flagpole" Wilson, who got his name shouting "Keep Bama white!" from atop a flagpole during University of Alabama race riots in 1956; and the CCC's national leader, St. Louis personal injury lawyer Gordon Baum.

Having made his CCC kick-off speech and after having met its members, Wallace, told the media: "There is nothing hateful about those people I've seen." While the prospective lieutenant governor should have been at the forefront of criticizing the CCC, Wallace instead ran to their podium and rallied them into their new year of white domination work. By doing so George Wallace, Jr. lent legitimacy to the CCC's racist screeds.

Unfortunately for Wallace, his CCC appearances did not help him at all. The natural question, after all, was: Is George Wallace a dues-paying member of the white supremacy group or is he simply the racists' source of inspiration? How could George Wallace, Jr. possibly win a statewide election now?

Here comes John McCain to support another white supremacist. Just five months after Wallace's latest, greatest speech for the CCC, McCain announced that he would endorse Wallace in the Republican primary for lieutenant governor.

In 1999, the SPLC had published an exposé on the CCC. As a result, the Republican National Committee warned Republican elected officials to avoid the CCC. John McCain knew of Wallace's close ties to the CCC. Before McCain officially endorsed Wallace, McCain was confronted by the media on this issue. McCain's campaign released a statement claiming that Wallace was "an enlightened progressive leader who always speaks of tolerance."

Like my 5th grade English teacher used to say, "That old dog won't hunt."

There are over 500,000 popularly elected political offices in the United States. There are nearly 20,000 elected state positions. Why did John McCain care so much about the lieutenant governorship of Alabama? There were far more important races going on in the nation. The U.S. House of Representatives and Senate elections were of extreme importance, as the Democratic Party was threatening to take control of both houses. There were more important states for McCain to campaign in, and there was a greater chance of making a difference if he campaigned for someone running for *national* office.

Of all the hundreds of thousands of Republicans running for office, Wallace may have been the only one who, in full view of the public, attended hate group meetings. Assuming that McCain believed that the nation's well-being hinged on who held the office of lieutenant governorship of Alabama, why did he insist on campaigning for George Wallace, Jr. rather than the other three Republican candidates? Why didn't John McCain wait until a Republican had been nominated for the office? Why did he have to involve himself in the extremely obscure primary process for the Alabama lieutenant governorship?

Why did McCain support the most racist candidate out of all the Republican and Democratic candidates? Why did he support the candidate that hate groups supported? Why did he support a candidate that was almost destined to lose because of his association with white supremacist hate groups? Why didn't McCain endorse Luther Strange, a Republican with no connections with hate groups?

No one outside of Alabama was at all interested in the Republican primary race that Wallace was running in. The only people outside of Alabama paying any attention to this primary race were hate groups and people who oppose hate groups.

I wonder which group John McCain belongs to.

McCain's men organized a major fundraiser for George Wallace, Jr. in January 2006. Alabamans hoping to meet McCain paid $250 per person to attend and paid $1000 per photograph taken with McCain and Wallace.

In his speech, McCain called Wallace a "good and decent American" who wanted to broaden the Republican base. One might ask, "Broaden the Republican base to include whom?"

McCain gave speeches in three Alabama cities for Wallace, bringing much-needed media attention to the controversial figure. It was a double-win for Wallace. For those Alabamans who assumed that McCain was not a racist, McCain's endorsement was likely a positive for Wallace. The only Alabamans who knew of McCain's connection with the white supremacist Richard Quinn and the *Southern Partisan* were probably racists themselves, so McCain's endorsement was a positive for them too.

Despite the best efforts of McCain's "outside agitation," Wallace lost the Republican primary election to attorney Luther Strange. McCain lucked out. Had Wallace won, McCain would have been subject to greater scrutiny of his controversial endorsement of Wallace.

Unsurprisingly, McCain did not return to Alabama to campaign for the non-racist Luther Strange, who lost to the Democrat.

The importance of McCain's endorsement of George Wallace, Jr., has been underreported and underemphasized. *The only logical reason for McCain's unusual behavior is that he wanted to put a friend of white supremacy in office.*

Alabamans wouldn't have it. They may not ever again allow a white supremacist near the governor's office. Certainly not another "George Wallace." Although it was hardly noted in the national news, the rebuffing of George Wallace, the CCC, and John McCain was a step forward for the New South.

TERRY NELSON

After campaigning for George Wallace, McCain paid some attention to his own presidential campaign. In mid-March 2006, McCain hired Terry Nelson to serve as a senior adviser on his election team.

While serving as McCain's senior adviser, Terry Nelson created commercials for the Republican Party attacking Democrats running for Senate. Nelson had previously produced commercials for Senator George Allen, who had hung up his own Confederate flag, and who had *his own associations with the CCC.*

The busy Terry Nelson was also hired by Wal-mart to manufacture a "grass-roots" campaign called "Working Families for Wal-mart." Of course, if Terry Nelson is paid hundreds of thousands of dollars to "create" some sort of "front" organization for Wal-mart, then it is not a grass-roots campaign. It is a campaign to manipulate and deceive the public. But perhaps this is what Nelson is best at. Wal-mart's contract was with Terry Nelson's Crosslink Strategies firm, one of whose ad-makers — Chris LaCivita — helped create ads for Swift Boat Veterans for Truth in order to spread misinformation about Vietnam veteran John Kerry during his 2004 presidential campaign. LaCivita worked with the likes of Jerome Corsi, a powerful racist, homophobic right-winger who, evidenced by his posts on conservative websites, has a penchant for homo-erotic fantasies involving liberal senators such as John Kerry, Hellary Clinton (as he calls her), and Ted Kennedy.

But back to Terry Nelson, whose relationship with McCain intensifies from here. Still serving as a senior McCain adviser, Terry Nelson needed some way of doing a "swiftboat" attack on Harry Ford, who, if elected, would be the first African American senator in Tennessee since Reconstruction. To destroy Harold Ford, Nelson teamed up with Scott Howell, who was best known for "swiftboating" Vietnam veteran Max Cleland. Having lost three of his limbs already, Cleland was fully hatcheted by Howell's campaign attack ad which "morphed" together images of Cleland, Osama bin Laden, and Saddam Hussein.

Howell and Terry Nelson went for the ultimate tried-and-true in racist manipulation. The greatest racial fear, historically speaking, for white men in America, has been the fear of black men having sexual relations with white women. All men have sexual insecurities, and it is no different with white men. In fact, sexual insecurities and the need for sexual security have been at the heart of racism throughout the world for thousands of years. It is no wonder that the last laws of segregation to be rescinded were the laws preventing men of color from marrying white women. But how does one exploit these insecurities in a campaign ad? Aren't these ads supposed to be about policy issues?

Of course not. That's why the Republican Party (and McCain (?)) hired Terry Nelson and Scott Howell. They made the anti-Ford ad about race. They fanned fears that Ford might have sex with a white woman. Or worse yet, perhaps he has already had sex with a white woman! Or even worse, many white women! Or perhaps the worst of all, they liked it! A lot!

So what does Terry Nelson do? Nelson films a scantily-dressed blonde woman holding her fingers up to her lips and ear and whispering, "Harold, call me."

This is simply the last segment of the anti-Ford ad. What is just as sinister is that Terry Nelson made the commercial seem as if average everyday Tennessee folks were being interviewed "on the street," so to speak. In fact, all of the people in the ad were actors. To make sure that the viewer got the point, Terry Nelson had a white actress early in the ad say, "Harold Ford looks nice. Isn't that enough?"

Hundreds of black men have been lynched by white mobs, and most of those men were beaten, stripped, castrated, burned, and hung because they were accused of having relations with, or raping, a white woman. The most famous case was that of Emmitt Till, who was fourteen-years-old. Till made some remark or whistled at a white woman in Mississippi. The boy was beaten to the extreme. The white men who murdered Emmitt mutilated his face and then tied him to a large weight and threw him in a river. His horrifying open-casket funeral helped spark the modern civil rights movement.

Fanning the racial-sexual fears and hatreds of white people is, as Terry Nelson knows, an extremely effective way of moving people. Since lynching is no longer legal, Nelson expected white men to instead vote Harold Ford into oblivion. They did, and Ford lost his Senate election.

But many people considered Nelson's ad racist, and there developed a true grass-roots campaign to have Nelson fired from his Wal-mart "grass roots" campaign. After people nationwide sent letters of concern to Wal-mart, the corporation decided to fire Terry Nelson. Here's some money; don't stand so close to us.

Nelson, who may or may not have felt disgraced, must have known he was in trouble now. He had earned a reputation as a racist or a purveyor of racism.

In comes John McCain. He seems drawn to racists in trouble.

In October 2006, Terry Nelson was fired by Wal-mart. In a matter of weeks, Nelson was promoted from senior adviser to the *national campaign manager* for the McCain presidential campaign. Perhaps McCain had fantasies of Terry Nelson doing to Barack Obama what Nelson had done to Harold Ford. Or perhaps a quick "swiftboating" of Hillary Clinton was in order.

John McCain has never publicly stated that he hates black people. But McCain is at most only one or two degrees removed from those who do.

Chapter 13
John McCain Seeks
John Hagee's Blessing

"I thank you for your spiritual guidance to politicians like
me who need it fairly often." John McCain, speaking to
Pastor John Hagee, July 2007.

San Antonio mega-church pastor John Hagee first established Christians
United for Israel in February 2006. The organization was formed to
transform Christian support for Jewish people into moneys and political aid
for right-wing Israeli politicians. Among the notions that CUFI has promoted
is that the city of Jerusalem should remain 100% in the hands of the Israeli
government, essentially ensuring that no peace deal between Palestinians
and Israelis can ever be signed.

(Hundreds of thousands of Christian and Muslim Palestinians fled
Jerusalem and Israel out of fear when the Israeli government took control
some sixty years ago. Most hoped to return to their homes in places like east
Jerusalem, but most could not. Their homes were taken over by the Israeli

government and are now occupied. A viable peace agreement would likely grant an autonomous region to Muslims and Christians in East Jerusalem.)

The apocalyptic vision of Pastor Hagee seems to push him to lobby for the end of the world, as the Bible prophesizes. Not long after Hagee formed CUFI, he got John McCain to jump aboard his campaign. McCain met with Hagee in January 2007, and Hagee announced that McCain "got it."

McCain then spoke at a CUFI event in July. He showered praise upon Pastor Hagee before launching into a Hagee-esque speech that was as hawkish as any McCain had ever given. Hagee must have been pleased with McCain's support and legitimization of CUFI and its cause. When McCain asked for Hagee's endorsement, Hagee granted his blessing upon the McCain campaign.

McCain, through his meeting with Hagee, his praise, and his appearance at the Hagee event, had essentially endorsed Hagee.

And when the secrets of McCain's beloved pastor came out in 2008, McCain openly confessed to George Stephanapolous on national television that McCain had actively solicited Hagee for his endorsement.

McCain did not need the pastor's endorsement. There are many non-controversial, normal pastors whose endorsement McCain could have sought. There are even many wealthy and powerful pastors who McCain could have courted, pastors who do not openly express hatred for various groups of God's children.

But McCain, *knowing* Hagee's views *and having given a speech* for Hagee's political action organization, *specifically chose* Pastor John Hagee to endorse McCain.

But Pastor John Hagee was openly and virulently anti-Catholic, anti-Muslim, anti-gay, and anti-women. It was well-published and well-known. Why would John McCain seek the endorsement of such a pastor when there are so many normal, non-hateful pastors out there with similar numbers of supporters and money?

The only possible explanation is that McCain wanted to ally himself with Hagee *because of Hagee's beliefs*. After all, Hagee's hateful and warmongering messages are consistent with McCain's personal tilt.

WOMEN, JEWS, MUSLIMS, CATHOLICS

John Hagee on women: "Do you know the difference between a woman with PMS and a snarling Doberman pinscher? The answer is lipstick. Do you know the difference between a terrorist and a woman with PMS? You can negotiate with a terrorist." [cited in Sarah Posner's *God's Profits: Faith, Fraud and the Republican Crusade for Values Voters*]

McCain also has a habit of trampling on the dignity of women, mostly through cruel words. He reportedly called his wife Cindy a "cunt" in public and implied that she dressed like a prostitute. McCain also had no objections when one of his supporters called Hillary Clinton a "bitch."

McCain seems to have no problem with intimidating female reporters who write the wrong things about him; this last habit is documented in *Free Ride*, and a careful accounting of the many reporters McCain has accosted seems to indicate that he especially disliked the female reporters.

Perhaps there is a bit of the misogynist in McCain, as evidenced by his cruel joke concerning Chelsea Clinton. At a 1998 Republican fundraiser, McCain asked the audience, "Why is Chelsea Clinton so ugly? Because her mother is Hillary Clinton and her father is Janet Reno." Chelsea Clinton had just turned eighteen at the time, which apparently for McCain, made her free game.

In April 2008, John McCain *opposed* a bill that prohibited employers from discriminating against women by paying them less than men working at the exact same position. McCain's excuse was that the law would bring about law suits, even though law suits are the only way women can prompt employers to pay equal salaries for equal work.

On Jews, Hagee blamed the Holocaust on Jews themselves:

> It was the disobedience and rebellion of the Jews, God's chosen people, to their covenantal responsibility to serve

only the one true God, Jehovah, that gave rise to the opposition and persecution that they experienced beginning in Canaan and continuing to this very day. . . Their
own rebellion had birthed the seed of anti–Semitism that
would arise and bring destruction to them for centuries to
come... it rises from the judgment of God upon his rebel-
lious chosen people (from Hagee's *Jerusalem Countdown*,
pp. 91–92).

On Iran, Hagee echoes McCain's own eagerness towards war with that
nation: "The coming nuclear showdown with Iran is a certainty," Hagee wrote
in 2006 in the Pentecostal magazine *Charisma*. "Israel and America must
confront Iran's nuclear ability and willingness to destroy Israel with nuclear
weapons. For Israel to wait is to risk committing national suicide." (cited in
The Nation, August 8, 2006)

On Muslims: In 2006, Hagee said on National Public Radio's *Fresh Air* that
"those who live by the Koran have a scriptural mandate to kill Christians
and Jews... it teaches that very clearly." He then alarmed listeners with the
following: "There are 1.3 billion people who follow the Islamic faith, so if
you're saying there's only 15 percent that want to come to America or invade
Israel to crush it, you're only talking about 200 million people. That's far
more than Hitler and Japan and Italy and all of the Axis powers in World War
II had under arms."

Hagee implies that there is a 100% probability that Iran will attack Israel
with nuclear weapons (even though they do not have such weapons) and
that the United States must protect Israel from annihilation. If, according to
Hagee, Muslims are called by God to kill Christians and Jews, then America
has no choice but to launch a preemptive military strike on Iran. This
predilection towards launching a military offensive against Iran matches
McCain's own desires, and McCain was not shy about his support for Hagee's
warmongering views concerning Israel: "And I am very proud of the Pastor
John Hagee's spiritual leadership to thousands of people and I am proud of
his commitment to the independence and the freedom of the state of Israel."

Hagee blamed Hurricane Katrina on those sinful New Orleans people, especially the gays, "The newspaper carried the story in our local area that was not carried nationally that there was to be a homosexual parade there on the Monday that the Katrina came. And the promise of that parade was that it was going to reach a level of sexuality never demonstrated before in any of the other Gay Pride parades. So I believe that the judgment of God is a very real thing. I know that there are people who demur from that, but I believe that the Bible teaches that when you violate the law of God, that God brings punishment sometimes before the Day of Judgment." On NPR's *Fresh Air* (9/18/06), then, Hagee had warned Americans that sinful cities will be destroyed by God. Presumably, then, Oklahomans, who are consistently hit by deadly tornadoes, are among the most sinful people in America.

Hagee's antipathy toward the Catholic Church has been widely discussed in the media. He's said many interesting things about the Catholic Church — far too many to print here. Here is the gist. Hagee wrote on the Catholic Church: "A Godless theology of hate that no one dared try to stop for a thousand years produced a harvest of hate."(from Hagee's book, *Should Christians Support Israel?*)

Is John McCain anti-Catholic, or does he simply seek the support of a major anti-Catholic activist? When George W. Bush spoke at Bob Jones University in South Carolina, McCain called Bush's actions "racist" and in the following Michigan primary, McCain's campaign called Catholics and gave them this alarming message: "Several weeks ago, Governor Bush spoke at Bob Jones University in South Carolina. Bob Jones has made strong anti-Catholic statements, including calling the pope the anti-Christ, the Catholic Church a satanic cult! John McCain, a pro-life senator, has strongly criticized this anti-Catholic bigotry, while Governor Bush has stayed silent while seeking the support of Bob Jones University. Because of this, one Catholic pro-life congressman has switched his support from Bush to McCain, and many Michigan Catholics support John McCain for president."

At the time of Bush's Bob Jones visit, McCain had also called the televangelist Jerry Falwell an agent of intolerance. And he was. Falwell claimed that September 11 was a punishment for the acts of American feminists, gays, and lesbians, as well as the ACLU. But after McCain lost the Republican nomination to George W. Bush, McCain actively sought the support of Jerry Falwell. The two met to create a renewed alliance. He also said that he would be open to speaking at Bob Jones University.

It seems that McCain's year 2000 stand against intolerant, hateful preachers was the exception that makes the rule. For a short period of time, McCain tried to distinguish himself from George Bush, who associated himself with an anti-Catholic university. But McCain returned to Bush's position after he lost the 2000 nomination. So, for a year or so, McCain spoke out against intolerant preachers, and after that, he returned to embracing them. Those hatemongering preachers like Hagee seem to represent McCain's core position.

After confirming that McCain had actively sought an alliance with John Hagee, George Stephanopoulos asked John McCain if he would now cut off ties with Hagee. McCain answered, "I'm glad to have his endorsement. I condemn remarks that are, in any way, viewed as anti-anything. But thanks for asking." McCain laughed.

Simple Thinking, Complex World, Easy Wars

"War hawk": One who advocates war; a hawk.

"We will win this conflict. We will win it easily." —John McCain on the Iraq War.

"I gotta give you some straight talk, my friends.... There's going to be other wars." —John McCain claiming that there will be new wars after the Iraq War.

The most eager and confident war hawks are the ones who hold racial biases. Racism allows hawks to argue for the killing of other people because those people being killed are seen as less than human, or at least less human than them.

Racists and hawks tend to flock together. Not only that, they tend to be one and the same. Not surprisingly, they share certain traits. One of these is the possession of a simplistic world view. This worldview tends to be divided into "us" and "them." Black and white. Good and evil. "You're either for us, or against us," as President George W. Bush said. "They" want to defeat, kill, oppress, rule, rape, exterminate, overwhelm, genetically alter, or harmfully change "us." "We" must stop them by starting a war, by bombing, by torturing, by any means necessary. After all, "they" will destroy "us."

While "we" may see ourselves as a complex and diverse group, "they" are almost always simplified, reduced, caricatured, and stereotyped. "They" are evil. "They" are all Communists. "They" subscribe to terrorism. "Their" religion makes them do bad things. "They" don't value life, not even their own. "They" are uncivilized and need us to rule them. "They" give in to their own passions, and that will hurt us. "They" are a ruthless people. "They" cannot be trusted.

This simplification of "them" allows people to believe that the war itself will be easily won. After all, if the enemy people are simple formulas, their society rather homogenous, their political economy structured in a rudimentary fashion, if their religion consists of a few basic rules and rituals, and if they seek some savior on a white horse (such as we are), then we will be welcomed as liberators. We know what's right for us *and* for them. Peace and justice and a U.S.-allied democratic government will blossom naturally, like wildflowers in a virgin meadow, after we bomb that meadow.

Their society and culture being so simple, it is also easy to envision a strategy for success. A three-step program for conquering a two-step society.

It is not a coincidence that America tends to start wars with peoples who are completely unfamiliar to Americans and their leaders. When the United States invaded the Philippines in 1898, there were essentially zero Filipinos in the United States. Same with Korea in 1950. Vietnam in 1965. Iraq in 1990. Remember Granada? Sending the Marines into Lebanon. Bombing Libya and Kosovo. Not many Panamanians in the U.S. in 1989, when we invaded and killed thousands of civilians there.

When the U.S. sponsored death squads in El Salvador, no one in the U.S. had ever eaten a pupusa. When the U.S. bombed Cambodia into a chaos that led to genocide, the only Southeast Asians in the United States were almost all Thai. When the U.S. supported Saddam Hussein in his chemical decimation of the Kurdish people, few Americans had ever met an Iraqi or a Kurd. When the U.S. ushered in torturer supreme General Pinochet, few Americans knew where Chile was located on a map. Overthrow democracy in Guatemala? Where's that? Terrorists in Nicaragua? Back then, the vast majority of Latinos in the U.S. were Mexicans, Puerto Ricans, and Cubans. Death squads and mass slaughter in Honduras, Indonesia, and Angola — but aren't they just tribal peoples?

There were two levels of simplification regarding the lead-up to war in Iraq. One level was the simplistic thinking of the right-wing hawks. The second level was the simplification of "information" provided for consumption by the American public.

In 1998, John McCain's foreign policy chief, Randy Scheunemann, drafted for Senator Trent Lott the "Iraq Liberation Act." McCain co-sponsored the bill, which was passed and signed into law by President Clinton. The law made "regime change" a goal of U.S. policy and prepared the U.S. for the Iraq War.

The act allocated money for a shady organization known as the Iraqi National Congress, which, of course, lobbied for a U.S. invasion of Iraq. The Iraqi National Congress was a London-based exile group run by Ahmed Chalabi. The INC had been sponsored by the CIA, but the intelligence agency stopped funding the INC in 1997, noting that Chalabi could not be trusted. The Iraq Liberation Act granted $33 million to Chalabi, but the State Department broke off relations when it found financial improprieties. Most importantly, the Clinton administration did not cave into McCain, neoconservative activists, or lobbyists; it never launched a full-out invasion of Iraq.

Later in 1998, McCain kicked off his presidential campaign, during which he pledged to "immediately" start armed insurrections in Iraq, Libya, and North Korea. Ironically, George W. Bush during the 2000 presidential campaign seemed much less interested in invading other nations and "nation-building" as he called it.

The terror attacks of September 11 provided a tremendous opportunity for right-wing hawks. In the days following the attacks, the hawks began setting up lobbying organizations designed to bring about an American war in Iraq. Randy Scheunemann (McCain's foreign policy man) organized the Committee for the Liberation of Iraq; it's not clear if Scheunemann consulted with McCain before setting up this pro-war lobbying group or if McCain directed him to form the group. Whatever the case, McCain was named an "honorary chairman" of the group.

According to Jim Lobe of *Foreign Policy in Focus*, Scheunemann teamed up with a former Lockheed Corporation Vice-President named Bruce P. Jackson to steer the Committee for the Liberation of Iraq. Lockheed is a military contractor and benefits tremendously from U.S. wars and U.S. allocation of military aid to foreign armies and nongovernmental armed groups.

Members of the Committee signed letters to George W. Bush advocating for an Iraq invasion just eight days after September 11, 2001. (Lobe)

Less than a month after September 11, on December 6, 2001, McCain and nine other other congressional leaders delivered a letter to President Bush urging him to invade Iraq. At that time, the U.S. was still on the hunt for Osama bin Laden.

McCain later disputed the contention that a shift of focus toward Iraq allowed Osama bin Laden to sneak away.

McCain's and other right-wingers' lobbying seemed to have been tremendously effective. John McCain's policy of "rogue state rollback" was essentially adapted by the Bush administration. Some minor adjustments were made to the list of "rogue states." Libya was replaced by Iran. And rather than calling them "rogue states," Bush and Cheney called them the "Axis of Evil." What had been John McCain's hawkish fantasy was sent to the Pentagon as a plan of action to be implemented in at least three nations.

McCain's policy was implemented immediately. Utilizing his foreign policy man's law, the "Iraqi Liberation Act," funds were given to the Iraqi National Congress to start shooting and blowing things up in Iraq.

Simplistic thinking prefers propaganda over the truth. While the U.S. government paid the INC for "information," the CIA, among others, complained that the INC was providing propaganda, not intelligence. "Even as it prepares for war against Iraq, the Pentagon is already engaged on a second front: its war against the Central Intelligence Agency," wrote Richard Dreyfuss in *The American Prospect* on Dec. 16, 2002, "The Pentagon is bringing relentless pressure to bear on the agency to produce intelligence reports more supportive of war with Iraq," wrote Dreyfuss. "Morale inside the U.S. national-security apparatus is said to be low, with career staffers feeling intimidated and pressured to justify the push for war."

Regarding the Committee for the Liberation of Iraq, imagine this. A group of powerful white American men decide that they will "promote regional peace, political freedom and international security" by invading a nation. That nation is both foreign and made up of ethnic groups that have traditionally been oppressed and treated with utter callousness by America. The group of white men do not hail from that nation. The group of white men do not have strong connections with people from that nation. The group of white men do not seek out the advice of people from that nation, except for shady characters who have sought an American invasion of that nation for years. The group of white men, though, care so much for the people of that nation that they are willing to launch an invasion of that nation to overthrow their government for the purpose of "peace, freedom and security." These white men are among the right-wing hawks who sustained the government they now wish to overthrow. Although they care deeply about the people of this foreign nation, these men do not speak of how many of those foreign people will die in the invasion they plan. These foreign people have every reason to trust that these men from America are good men and all the carnage will be worth it.

Is there not either 1) a sense of "white man's burden" and colonial dominion or 2) a sense of pure exploitation of a group of people considered foreign and subhuman?

The simplistic thinking of the self-serving "savior" is matched by the simplistic thinking that the American people were expected to adapt.

It started with the invasion of Afghanistan. Americans were told that the Taliban and Al Qaeda were essentially one and the same. This allowed the Bush administration to invade Afghanistan with the goal of overthrowing the Taliban *instead of capturing Osama bin Laden*. Rather than focusing like a laser on Osama bin Laden, the vast majority of resources were spent fighting the Taliban, occupying large tracts of land and installing a new government.

When it was made public that Osama bin Laden could not be found in the Taliban government offices, the American public was led to believe that the U.S. government was nevertheless doing its best to capture Osama bin Laden. It was not. CIA agents and Northern Alliance officers on the ground reported that only a small number of American soldiers were assigned the task of capturing Osama bin Laden. Investigative reports by both the *Washington Post* and CNN confirmed that paltry military resources had been dedicated to the capture of Osama bin Laden. One pundit joked that U.S. forces had Osama bin Laden surrounded, on three of four sides. Even James Kagan, a foreign policy adviser for John McCain, admitted on *The Charlie Rose Show* on May 15, 2008 that the Republican administration had dedicated too few soldiers to hunt for Osama bin Laden; this allowed Osama bin Laden to escape.

A tremendous bomb called a "Daisy Cutter" was dropped on the mountains of Tora Bora, and the simple message conveyed to the American people was, "We are using every available resource to capture Osama bin Laden." But that was an illusion.

If the Bush administration and its head cheerleader John McCain had allocated as many resources to capturing or killing Osama bin Laden as it did invading Iraq, then the father figure of Al Qaeda would have been captured in 2001 or 2002. And the hawks would have had no excuse to invade Iraq.

Instead, after Osama bin Laden "escaped" from the small contingent of U.S. forces, he suddenly became low priority. Instead, we were told, the war on terror must be fought against the rogue states of Iraq, Iran, and North Korea.

Bush and McCain supposedly led a "war on terror." But the Bush–McCain war on terror did not target terrorists. It targeted *nations*. I am not advocating for war here, but a *true* war on terror would be fought against, say, Al Qaeda, Hezbollah, and Hamas. We might consider capturing the Mexican drug lords responsible for so many deaths along the Texas border. We might throw homegrown terrorists like the KKK on the list of terrorists.

A nonviolent war against terror might involve negotiating with various parties, including those among the "Axis of Evil": Iran and North Korea. And those not yet on that Axis: Syria, Palestine, Lebanon, etc. It might involve asking Israel not to bomb civilians in Lebanon or to take it easy on the people they have living in that giant cage called "Gaza." It might involve serious negotiations with nations arming other nations and paramilitary groups. It might involve working to stop *any* proliferation of nuclear weapons rather than approving them for some nations and invading other nations for allegedly building them.

Because Bush and McCain acted as if there were no question that this is how a war on terror should be fought — against nations we don't like — the American people went along. In reality, blowing up secular governments like Saddam Hussein's was precisely what "Islamic fascists" prayed for every day. In such a state of fear were Americans — hearing reports of attempted terror attacks every month or so — that easy, simplistic answers were eagerly swallowed up. "Don't worry about the actual terrorists," the public were told. "Let's attack these national governments instead. That will take care of the terrorists."

The left–wing was guilty, too, of simplistic thinking. Liberals claimed that resources were taken away from the hunt for bin Laden in order to fight the Iraq War. No, the United States could have easily funded and supplied both. If George Bush had said, "We need to increase taxes and draft young soldiers in order to capture Osama bin Laden," the American people would have gladly sacrificed whatever necessary.

But the American people would *not* sacrifice anything and everything to invade Iraq.

Furthermore, if Osama bin Laden had been captured, then the American people would have felt almost no desire to invade Iraq. "We've captured Osama bin Laden already. We caught the man responsible for September 11. Why do we need to invade Iraq for?"

Not capturing Osama bin Laden served two purposes. First, it kept alive the atmosphere of fear in the United States. Osama bin Laden gets on TV every few months and prods Americans' anxiety and loathing. The knowledge that "he's still out there," makes us think of the twin towers collapsing, the Pentagon burning. Second, Osama's continued existence provided reason for invading Iraq. And it became a self-fulfilling prophecy. Our invasion brought about a civil war, which allowed an "Al Qaeda in Iraq" to establish itself.

"You see why we needed to invade Iraq?" we were then told. "Because Al Qaeda is here in Iraq."

It was not surprising that many Americans had adapted the simplistic thinking of the Bush–McCain leadership. It is easy to mold public opinion when that public had been trained to think over the years in the most simplistic terms. Manifest Destiny meant that we should bulldoze whatever civilization stands in the way of expanding the American nation. Carnage galore of every sort is acceptable in the worldwide war against Communism.

Trust the government's strategy for the war on terror because they have classified information that you don't have.

Two plus two is five. Just accept it.

Most mainstream media have characterized John McCain as a free-thinker or maverick within the Republican Party. Indeed, a frank counterbalance to the quickening drums of war would have been a vital service to our democracy. Even a voice utilizing just slightly more sophisticated thinking than Dick Cheney's rhetoric would have provided sorely needed brain activity.

But McCain was just the opposite. He led the charge to go to war in Iraq with simplistic cheers and chants.

When the likes of Vice-President Dick Cheney said that Iraq was partially responsible for the attacks of September 11, 2001, John McCain quietly "doubted" this untrue assertion. What a maverick. Regarding Saddam Hussein, McCain trumped up pure conjecture into "truth" as the *LA Times* reported:

> "He [Saddam] has developed stocks of germs and toxins in sufficient quantities to kill the entire population of the Earth multiple times," McCain said, according to the Congressional Record. "He has placed weapons laden with these poisons on alert to fire at his neighbors within minutes, not hours, and has devolved authority to fire them to subordinates. He develops nuclear weapons with which he would hold his neighbors and us hostage."

Of course, all of this was a severe twist of the truth. McCain aide Mark Salter admitted to reporters that McCain had only read the *summary* of the National Intelligence Estimate sent to Congress. The full report explained that none of what McCain had stated was actually *known to be true* by American intelligence. What had been described in the summary was only a possibility, not a reality, the body of the work explained. But McCain did not read the body of the work.

He merely projected his hawkish fantasy to the world as truth.

McCain said of the prospects for a successful military campaign: "I believe that the success will be fairly easy." Four months later, in January 2003, he repeated, "We will win this conflict. We will win it easily." McCain applied the word "win" to a war, as if it were a video game. And to say, "We will win it easily" was either a conscious distortion of the truth or an almost willful self-deception of a man who seeks to simplify difficult issues. (see *Free Ride*)

How easy would it be? McCain claimed that the invasion and occupation would require less than 100,000 soldiers. Of course this was way off, and soon after the occupation began, McCain began demanding that troop levels be increased tremendously.

On MSNBC's *Hardball*, Chris Matthews asked John McCain just one week before the invasion, "Do you believe that the people of Iraq or at least a large number of them will treat us as liberators?" This question should have elicited a nuanced and complex answer. For instance, McCain could have said that we will be seen as liberators if we do not resemble previous European colonizers. He could have said that those who prefer an Islamic government are more likely to see us as occupiers than liberators. John McCain answered, "Absolutely. Absolutely." (See *Free Ride*, page 142)

McCain's answer reveals that he had simplified Iraqi society and Iraqi political culture. But this was the habit of Bush and McCain. According to some, Bush, before the invasion, did not know there was a difference between Sunni and Shiite Muslims.

When the American invasion began, John McCain argued that anti-war protests in the U.S. should stop "Because, you know, there comes a time for debate and discussion and protests, and then there comes a time when we should rally behind the president and the troops when we go into a conflict."

"Look," McCain said, "it's not possible to only support the troops and not their mission." Here was the "dissent is unpatriotic (or even treasonous)" message McCain promoted after the Vietnam War, and his unconditional support for Bush's war in Iraq paralleled his support for Nixon's expanding war in Southeast Asia. "Shut up, we're the good guys," seems to be McCain's simplistic attitude. (quote cited in *Free Ride*, page 143)

McCain is a true believer of the vision of Theodore Roosevelt. McCain believes that we are ordained by God Himself to bring democracy to the world. It is "providence," he says, that we do so. We are "the New Jerusalem," he says. And he implies that war and violence may be a part of this, our "sacred duty," as he calls it.

In a speech to the University of Southern California on March 25, 2002, he declared that "We [Americans] are part of something providential: a great experiment to prove to the world that democracy is not only the most effective form of government, but the only moral government." Spoke McCain:

> Theodore Roosevelt is one of my greatest political heroes.
> The "strenuous life" was T.R.'s definition of Americanism,
> a celebration of America's pioneer ethos, the virtues that

had won the West and inspired our belief in ourselves as the New Jerusalem, bound by sacred duty to *suffer hardship and risk danger* to protect the values of our civilization and impart them to humanity. "We cannot sit huddled within our borders," he warned, "and avow ourselves merely an assemblage of well-to-do hucksters who care nothing for what happens beyond."

In this speech, McCain invokes the spirit of Teddy Roosevelt more than once. Teddy Roosevelt is John McCain's hero and model president. The connection goes beyond McCain being inspired by Teddy Roosevelt's military adventures and his civilian life. McCain's grandfather, Slew McCain, fought under Teddy Roosevelt as he charged into the Philippines to commence the bloody American conquest of the people there. In many ways, Slew McCain and Teddy Roosevelt helped to invent the word "gook" and John McCain carried forth the tradition.

So, if McCain consistently mentions Teddy Roosevelt as the model for meeting our "sacred duty to suffer hardship and risk danger to protect the values of our civilization and *impart them to humanity*," then what can we learn from Teddy Roosevelt about our "sacred duty" as the "New Jerusalem"? Roosevelt declared:

> The most ultimately righteous of all wars is a war with savages, though it is apt to be also the most terrible and inhuman… It is of incalculable importance that America, Australia, and Siberia should pass out of the hands of the red, black, and yellow aboriginal owners, and become the heritage of the dominant world races.

Here, Roosevelt states that it is the moral obligation of Americans to wage war against those people we consider savages. We must take land and power out of the hands of these "red, black, and yellow" aborigines and put that land and power into the hands of the white man. (see Welch, *Myth of the Maverick*)

John McCain seems to confess to the maniacal desire of his hero for expanding the American empire through the most brutal and sickening military means:

> Some critics, in his day and ours, saw in Roosevelt's patriotism only flag-waving chauvinism, not all that dissimilar to Old World ancestral allegiances that incited one people to subjugate another and plunged whole continents into war. But they did not see the universality of the ideals that formed his creed.

According to McCain what made Roosevelt's brutal imperialism okay was the universality of Roosevelt's ideals. McCain said that "through the years, generation after generation of Americans has held fast to the belief that we were meant to transform history." We are to "prove to the world" that democracy is the "most effective" and "most moral" form of government.

How does McCain propose to fulfill our "sacred duty" to "impart our values" upon the rest of the world? In his USC speech, he does not mention anything about creating a more perfect union here in the United States. In fact, he bemoans Americans for their desire for "luxuries" and their obsession over their own rights. We should be living "strenuous lives" by reaching out into the world and doing something out there and avoid being "hucksters" isolated from other nations.

In his speech, McCain spoke of a terribly dangerous effort to reach the South Pole. Whatever the cost of that dangerous mission, he intoned, it was well worth it, as that effort gave those who survived meaning in their lives. McCain spoke of elderly veterans on the verge of death:

> But as they reach the end of their days, the accomplishments or disappointments of their peacetime years don't seem all that important to them. The memories of personal triumphs aren't an adequate account of their long years. It is the memory of war they return to, the memory of war that gave their lives lasting meaning. They return to hard times, times of pain, suffering, loss, violence and fear.

They return to the place where they risked everything, absolutely everything, for the country that sent them there. No later success ever outshone its glory, or later defeat taken it from them. It is still there and vivid at the moment of their last breath.

It is *war* that gives their lives lasting meaning.

McCain does not say it out loud, but all of the clues are there: Teddy Roosevelt is his model. War and painful efforts give our lives meaning. We must fulfill our "sacred duty" beyond our borders. *War is the way we impart our values on humanity.*

During his current run for president, though, he has spoken more explicitly about his plans. On January 27, 2008, McCain revealed more about our upcoming work to fulfill our "sacred duty":

> I gotta give you some straight talk, my friends. This is a tough war we're in. It's not going to be over right away. There's going to be other wars. I'm sorry to tell you. There's going to be other wars. We will never surrender but there will be other wars. We're going to have a lot of PTSD, my friends...

McCain was speaking in Polk City, Florida about the conditions at Veterans Administration hospitals. Broadcast on CNN, McCain was essentially warning Americans that these hospitals will have to improve, as many more Americans will be returning from wars to be started in the near future.

Perhaps because McCain is so sure that there will be more wars, he has spoken about expanding the military and even creating new branches of the military. According to Welch, he wants to expand the standing Army and Marines by 20%, create a new OSS organization to fight wars using unusual tactics, and create an "Army Advisor Corps" to help foreign armies around the world in their military operations. How will he accomplish this?

By encouraging Americans to give up seeking "luxuries," as he puts it, and to live a "strenuous life" in "proving" democracy "most moral." But that might not be enough, so John McCain has toyed with the idea of reinstating the military draft. "While the volunteer military has been successful, fewer Americans know and appreciate the sacrifices and contributions of their fellow citizens who serve in uniform. The military is suffering severe recruitment problems... " McCain writes, "The decline of the citizen–soldier is not healthy for a democracy. While it is not currently politically practical to revive the draft, it is important to find better incentives and opportunities for more young Americans to choose service in the military, if not for a career, then at least for a limited period of time." (Welch, 169-170)

It sounds like McCain would start drafting young men and women into the armed services if it were "politically practical." Whether or not there is a draft, it tends to be people of color who end up in the military, whether it is because they suffer higher rates of poverty or because they need to get a green card. At the other end of the missiles, the people who die from these wars that McCain foresees will almost certainly be people of color too.

Those military contractors, politicians, and large shareholders who benefit the most will be mostly wealthy Americans. Mostly white.

Teddy Roosevelt would salute McCain with a cannon blast, maybe fired at his favorite targets: the Philippines, Cuba (long before Castro), Panama, and China.

Speaking of "easy" wars, the easiest way of fighting a war is by arming someone else and having them fight the war. This is done by sending guns, planes, ships, missiles, and money to various armed groups, governments, and dictators. The U.S. has supported such parties as Osama bin Laden and Al Qaeda, Saddam Hussein, Manuel Noreiga, Saudi Arabia, the Communist Party of China, the "Islamic fascists" of Iran, the dictators of El Salvador, Honduras, Guatemala, Chile, Argentina, Haiti, and other Latin American countries; dictators in Nigeria and other African nations; and so on and so on. Of course, the U.S. has little control over these parties, and they often go on killing sprees that may garner *more* U.S. support or may inspire the U.S. to start a shooting war with them. Such wars, of course, require American women and men to sacrifice their lives. It is incredible then, that these violent parties continue to squeeze billions of dollars from the U.S. government. How do they do it?

They hire lobbyists to run campaigns in the United States. These campaigns are designed to spread propaganda and disinformation and persuasive arguments in order to "educate" presidents, senators, and congressmen. These lobbyists are highly skilled and have cost the lives of thousands of Americans and millions of non-Americans.

John McCain has hired these same lobbyists to run his 2008 campaign.

Hired as the chief political strategist for John McCain, Charlie Black has lobbied for dictators Ferdinand Marcos of the Philippine Islands; Mohamed Siad Barre of Somalia; and Mobuto Sese Seko of Zaire. They are each responsible for 10,000s or 100,000s of violent deaths in their own nations. Highlights include the following. Marcos murdered and tortured his opposition while his wife, Imelda Marcos, hoarded perhaps the largest shoe collection in the world. Siad Barre's army in Somalia killed 40,000 to 50,000 unarmed civilians from June 1988 to January 1990. The vicious nature of his rule led to the national chaos of Somalia in the early 1990s, which resulted in the starvation of 100,000s of Somalis. That led to George H.W. Bush's military intervention aimed at bringing order and food to the Somali population. This ended with the killing of 18 American Marines in Mogadishu, which was considered a great triumph among anti-U.S. Islamic armed groups of various stripes. And that success emboldened terrorists to organize attacks against, among other targets, the World Trade Center.

One of the worst cleptocrats in the world was Mobuto Sese Seko. Besides ruling brutally over Zaire, Mobuto regularly stole major portions of that nation's wealth. Meanwhile, millions of Zaire's children starved to death. What did Mobuto do with all that money? One million dollars a year went to Charlie Black.

Charlie Black was not averse to helping terrorist organizations such as Jonas Savimbi's UNITA guerilla group in Angola, who lined Charlie Black's pockets with hundreds of thousands of dollars. Here is a little something the *New York Times* reported on Savimbi's decades of terror:

Mr. Savimbi personally beat to death a rival's wife and children. He also shelled civilians, sowed land mines and then bombed a Red Cross–run factory making artificial legs for victims of mines. "We have to call him Africa's classical terrorist," said Makau Mutua, a professor of law and Africa specialist. "In the history of the continent, I think he's unique because of the degree of suffering he caused without showing any remorse." (March 2, 2002)

Charlie Black is just one of John McCain's lobbyist/campaign organizers, and I've only summarized three of his client dictators/terrorists. Others include the dictators of Nigeria and Equatorial Guinea.

I have not listed all of the lobbyists for foreign regimes that McCain has hired for his campaign. Others include Frank Donatelli, Rick Davis, Kevin Fray, Peter Madigan, Wayne Berman, and Kirsten Chadwick. They lobbied for some of the most brutal dictators in the world and then found themselves offered a job by John McCain. They are to do for McCain what they did for the guerilla leaders: burnish his rough image and help him seize power.

There are some governments and terrorist groups who even the United States won't throw money at. One of this exclusive bunch is the military junta ruling over Myanmar (formerly Burma). With an iron fist, the junta has killed their enemies and run entire ethnic groups into the rainforest, or out of it. They have terrorized Nobel Peace Prize winner Aung San Suu Kyi and kept her imprisoned and silenced. Their latest and most incredible crime is to prevent food and medicine from reaching the millions of victims of Cyclone Nargis. As their people starve and die of disease in flooded, mud–soaked regions, the military junta has taken foreign food and medicine aid and hoarded it in their own warehouses.

Who would work for such a sick group of people? One such person is Doug Davenport, who was hired as McCain's campaign manager for the Mid–Atlantic States. Another is Doug Goodyear, hired as McCain's convention CEO.

The vast majority of McCain's lobbyist-organizers' victims are people of color. This is not a coincidence. Would McCain's lobbyists work for these dictators if they were killing Canadians, Dutch people, the Irish, or Italians? Possibly. Would McCain hire a lobbyist who had worked for Slobodan Milosevic? Or the Irish Republican Army? Or Hamas?

How does he justify hiring people who have worked for Jonas Savimbi or the Vietnamese Communist Party or alleged child enslavers in Dubai or those associated with the massacre-happy paramilitary groups of Colombia or Nigerian dictator Ibrahim Babangida?

How does he justify it? How does he do it?

In a complex world such as ours, simplistic thinking makes life, and war, easy.

The Final Word:
A John McCain Presidency

There are two brothers. One is named Johnny and the other Abel.

They play in the backyard. When their mother is not looking Johnny punches Abel in the stomach. Abel doubles over and says, "Stop that!" Abel tells their mother about Johnny, but their mother does not believe him.

So the next day, Johnny does the same thing. And the day after that. Again and again. Punching Abel's stomach.

One day Johnny's mother catches Johnny punching Abel. His mother tells Johnny to apologize. Johnny does not want to apologize. He says he hates Abel and will hate him as long as he lives.

His mommy tells Johnny that if he does not apologize he cannot be President of the Backyard. Johnny apologizes to Abel.

Johnny gets caught punching a neighborhood child in the stomach. Again, he is told to apologize or he cannot be President. So he apologizes.

Johnny punches cousins, sisters, dogs, and the mailman. Each time he is caught, he is told that if he wants to be President, he must apologize. And he does, sometimes with an eloquent speech.

As long as Johnny has a chance to be President of the Yard, he gladly apologizes, and then goes on with business as usual.

His mother worries that Johnny really does not care about his victims. Perhaps Johnny is just apologizing so he can be President. Perhaps when Johnny apologizes, he doesn't really mean it. She worries that Johnny's character really has not changed. He remains disturbingly callous. Oh well, she thinks, he's only going to be President.

John McCain has apologized, distanced himself from his friends, explained that he is not a racist, and asked his friends and associates to resign from his campaign. He has done all of this at a maddening pace.

He has almost retracted his entire personality.

He declared that he would continue using the racist epithet "gook" until he died, and then "apologized" for using the epithet. He supported the Confederate flag, and then apologized for supposedly lying about his support of the Confederate flag; he never actually apologized for supporting the Confederate flag. After seeking the endorsement of Reverend John Hagee, McCain then distanced himself from Hagee; then Hagee apologized for calling the Catholic Church "the Great Whore"; eventually McCain de-accepted Hagee's endorsement, and Hagee withdrew his endorsement anyway. McCain happily embraced the endorsement he sought from televangelist Rob Parsley and then distanced himself from him, going back and forth just as he had wholeheartedly embraced televangelist Jerry Falwell after he had called him an agent of intolerance.

McCain has distanced himself from his white supremacist buddies; they aren't behind the microphones anymore or standing next to McCain on the stump. But he still pays the worst white supremicist — Richard Quinn — hundreds of thousands of dollars for his services. Quinn is under investigation for election violations, but McCain has not fired him yet.

In his never-ending string of offenses and apologies, McCain even apologized in 2007 for using the term "tar baby," which is offensive to many African Americans; and among his most recent image revisions was his letting go of his race-baiting long-time helper Terry Nelson, who was his campaign manager; in this case, McCain did not tell Nelson to go away because Nelson was a racist. Rather, Nelson left because the campaign was being run into the ground. After McCain's campaign took off and he won the Republican nomination, he asked a couple of his most morally reprehensible lobbyist buddies to leave the campaign because his association with dictators and terrorists kinda made him look bad.

But Johnny only changes his image. He does not change his character. That is why he must regularly apologize for his actions and distance himself from his buddies.

Many writers have pointed out that McCain holds multiple positions on most major issues. Some writers like to point out John McCain's hypocrisies. Indeed, McCain is a major hypocrite on many issues, including his trademark issue, clean government.

The impression that these writers give is of a man who believes in nothing. There is no real McCain. He is the sum of his advisers; his belief system is "I wanna be president," and he is willing to say anything and do anything to become president. Of course, we have seen a great deal of this part of McCain's personality. His desire to be president seems to consume him, evidenced by his dancing from one position to the next, sometimes keeping a foot on two positions simultaneously.

But there is a core McCain.

He is a human being. He holds sincere beliefs and carries with him distorted understandings of the world. He has a particular worldview. He suffers from bouts of rage. Roiling within him are fears and insecurities, regrets and vengeance. There are some people and some things that he hates. Some that he holds dearly to heart. Memories rack him and come to the forefront of his mind.

Not all Vietnam veterans respond to their war experiences the same way. McCain's psychological response to his war, torture, and prison experiences defines his personality.

There are political points to be scored by pointing out McCain's hypocrisies, but in a McCain presidency, he will find no need to jump from one position to another, contradicting himself constantly. He will have the brass ring in hand. He will be able to be himself, finally. And what a liberation that will be.

How will the real, core McCain behave as president? That should be the question. That should also be a source of worry.

Perhaps unadulterated fright.

By studying the real, core McCain, we discover a consistent, disturbing racism. There are many, many racists in the world. Billions. But there is only one President of the United States, and before we make McCain the president, we must consider his particular brand of racism.

No American has ever consistently repeated the racist epithet "gook" for mass media broadcast. John McCain did so for the vast majority of his first presidential campaign.

No president has ever had such friendly relations with white supremacy groups. McCain would be the first president who represented a major step backwards in regards to this issue.

In addition to hate speech, John McCain's racism also expresses itself through 1) hiring various racist or race-baiting campaign managers and advisers, 2) his seeking the endorsements of racists, and 3) endorsing candidates that support hate groups and whites-only clubs.

What is peculiar about McCain's racism is that it is a *public* racism. His rage and resentment overflow into a defiant racist *pride*. *He wants us to know that he is racist.* He consorts with white supremacists and spits racial slurs with his eyes looking directly into the cameras.

In most cases, racism expressed in public is only the tip of the iceberg. That is, if a person is acting out in a racist manner in public, then in private that person is certainly even more racist.

The evidence is there — from McCain's supporting the rescinding of MLK Day to his stumping for a white supremacist candidate for state office — we simply cannot fathom exactly how deep the racism runs. As if it could be measured in feet or yards.

It cannot.

We can, however, make some educated guesses as to how a person with severe racial biases will behave as president of our nation.

"RECKLESS" FOREIGN POLICY

John McCain's racism is most dangerous when it expresses itself through foreign policy. His foreign policy is already geared toward "righting" the U.S. defeat in the Vietnam War. Add on top of that an apparent disregard for the lives of foreign peoples, and you get "rogue state rollback."

Recently John McCain called Barack Obama "reckless" for saying that he would be willing to communicate with Iran without "preconditions." Of course, liberal commentators pointed out that McCain himself said that he would speak with Hamas, an organization that the U.S. government considers terrorist. Yes, there is the flip–flopping McCain, again and again. Who is the real McCain?

It is revealing to examine the foreign policies that McCain *has not* called "reckless" over the decades. John McCain generally agreed with Reagan–Bush foreign policy, from the early 1980s to the end of that era in 1993. In those years, McCain did not call reckless Reagan and Bush's arming of Saddam Hussein. He did not protest when Donald Rumsfeld shook hands and improved relations with Saddam Hussein while Hussein was launching chemical weapons at the Kurdish people.

McCain did not call it "reckless" when the Reagan–Bush administration illegally negotiated with Muslim terrorists and then sold them arms. Perhaps this was not "reckless" because the money gained by those arms sales were illegally funneled to John McCain's beloved "contra" terrorists in Nicaragua.

McCain contributed his own money to the "contras," who were, as stated before, known for the most bizarre sado-sexual killings of civilians. Contra violence threatened to destabilize the entire region. Not "reckless."

McCain voted to send support to an alliance of armed groups in Cambodia that included the Khmer Rouge. This put Cambodia at risk of another genocide. Not "reckless."

McCain announced that as president, he would immediately arm groups to start insurrections in at least three nations and to back them up with American troops. Such announcements only encourage such nations as Iraq, Iran, Libya, North Korea, Syria, and Pakistan to try to build nuclear weapons and to test them. Their excuse (and possibly their sincere reason) for doing so is that they must defend their regime and their nation against a U.S. invasion. Not "reckless."

From one face, McCain claims that "speaking" to Iran is "reckless." From the other face, McCain is willing to negotiate with terrorists, and even arm them. The real McCain considers no foreign policy "reckless," as long as he can couch it in terms of a simplistic, black-and-white worldview that pits us versus them, good versus evil, America against the bad guys, with the far-right defining those terms.

This simplistic thinking is the hallmark of the Goldwater/Wallace mindset from which McCain seems to draw inspiration. Simplistic on race. Simplistic on war.

But even traditional conservatives were disturbed when McCain was caught singing, "Bomb, bomb, bomb, bomb, bomb Iran," to the tune of the Beach Boys' "Barbara Ann."

How many new wars will John McCain start as a president?

In my estimation, John McCain is more likely than the vast majority of elected officials to use all-out war as a tool of negotiation with foreign entities. Those entities might be national governments or terrorist groups. Of course, as a senator, McCain was only in the position to advocate for those violent activities. As the president and Commander in Chief, McCain could make reality his visions of war. When asked by an urgent and insistent Commander in Chief, Congress rarely refuses a president his war powers.

John McCain this year declared openly that there will be more wars.

By calling off the hunt for Osama bin Laden, the Republican Party essentially reserved a future war for the United States. The question is, when will this war action commence?

The hunt for bin Laden may provide an "October Surprise" for John McCain; that is, if McCain needs a boost before the 2008 presidential election, Bush can send a team in to finally kill or capture Osama bin Laden, right before Americans begin voting. This surprise could win McCain the election.

Barack Obama has for months criticized the Republican Party for giving up the search for bin Laden. The Democratic Party has wondered out loud for years why we are not more aggressively searching for Osama bin Laden. Just months before early voting begins, McCain finally responded in May 2008, saying essentially that he would renew the search for Osama bin Laden. This in itself is a bit of a surprise.

A true "October Surprise" — a 2008 capture of Osama bin Laden in order to win the presidential election for McCain — is almost too crass to imagine. *Almost* too crass. The reason why the original "October Surprise" theory was put forth by Carter/Reagan aide Gary Sick was that it *is* plausible that a Republican Administration would delay the freeing of American hostages or delay the capture of Osama bin Laden in order to ensure election day victory.

Assuming that the renewed search for bin Laden does not occur until McCain is elected president, can President McCain commence such a search and destroy mission without starting a couple of wars? Bush started wars in Afghanistan and Iraq. He toyed with warring with Syria and Iran.

McCain was one of the progenitors behind Bush's bellicosity, Bush's "Axis of Evil" being an obvious adaptation of McCain's "rogue state rollback." And McCain's crew of neoconservative lobbyists played a major role in preparing the U.S. for a war in Iraq long before September 11, 2001.

Since Osama bin Laden is likely in Pakistan, the new war would likely be fought against that nation.

If the Pakistani government seems too democratic at the time of the desired invasion, McCain may negotiate an invasion in which the Pakistani and the U.S. governments form a military alliance and send troops into the regions of Pakistan where bin Laden is likely located.

Most likely, Pakistan will rebuff initial efforts by the U.S. to send American troops into Pakistan. In this case, McCain may consider the Pakistani government undemocratic. He may wish to "impart our values" upon that nation. McCain could use the argument he had developed for Bush's Axis of Evil: that Pakistan's nuclear bombs (developed with no real objections from the U.S.) represented a threat to U.S. national security. Furthermore, McCain could argue that Pakistan was harboring terrorists, namely Osama bin Laden.

There are many ways in which a war with Pakistan can be started. It may matter less what the official reasons are and more how the media campaign is conducted. McCain is a master of the media, and his lobbyist friends are paid huge money to conduct media campaigns, sometimes for extremely disturbing figures. Even George W. Bush was able to convince Americans to fight an unnecessary war in Iraq. I can think of no instance in recent history when a President demanding to commence a war was rebuffed, except one: Reagan's attempt to increase American military aid to the "contras" in Nicaragua. Americans and their Congress are easily seduced by war.

In 2000, McCain promised to "immediately" start and support armed insurrections in Iran, North Korea, and Libya. Although diplomacy and communication with these nations has been working, McCain has already said that he would place conditions on any communication with the Iranian regime. Furthermore, the classic McCain tempestuousness could result in our ceasing negotiations. Cessation of negotiations could be used as evidence that the "rogue state" was attempting to hide nuclear weapons — just like Saddam Hussein had supposedly done. The United States would then have to invade that nation in order to find and destroy those weapons of mass destruction, however imaginary they might be.

McCain could also start a new war by expanding a current war into new arenas. The war on terror can be expanded in many ways. The Bush administration toyed with the idea of warring with Syria. It gave Israel the green light to bomb Lebanon; if Israel needed help with that, it could draw the United States in, just like the U.S. was drawn into Vietnam by giving the French air support in their war to keep that nation part of the French empire. If Israel asked for the U.S. to help them fight a war, McCain seems he would be open to helping. McCain, with Hagee's spiritual guidance, seems cocked and ready for a just war in the "defense of Israel."

But the most obvious McCain war would be a war against Iran. He has already clamored that Iran is killing U.S. soldiers in Iraq. The murder of just one U.S. soldier triggered the U.S. invasion of Panama.

RELIGION AND WAR

The religious right would applaud an invasion of Iran. Pastor John Hagee declared in 2006:

> The United States must join Israel in a pre-emptive military strike against Iran to fulfill God's plan for both Israel and the West... a biblically prophesied end-time confrontation with Iran, which will lead to the Rapture, Tribulation, and Second Coming of Christ.

McCain spoke in mid-July 2007 at a Christians United for Israel conference organized by Pastor John Hagee:

> Thank you Pastor Hagee. Thank you, thank you all for being here. Thank you for your kind and generous welcome. Thank you Pastor Hagee. You and Diana are two of the most wonderful people I know. If you ever want to run for office in Israel I think you got a pretty good shot at it. And *I thank you for your spiritual guidance to politicians like me who need it fairly often.* It's very hard trying to do the Lord's work in the city of Satan, and I'm grateful to have you here [looks to crowd] and all of you here.

Interestingly, McCain in this speech seemed to add *Syria* to the list of "rogue states," "Axis of Evil," and "war on terror." He also said that he saw in Russia Premier Vladimir Putin's eyes only three letters: "KGB." McCain's wars were expanding, in his mind, and he even clued us in that Saudi Arabia may involve itself in an expanding Iraqi civil war.

McCain said with emphatic determination that the U.S. will not allow Iran to develop nuclear weapons and told the crowd that Iran was making progress toward making a nuclear weapon.

As chronicled by David Corn in *Mother Jones*, Reverend Ron Parsley wrote about the religion of Islam in his book *Silent No More*. The title of the chapter was "The Deception of Allah":

> I cannot tell you how important it is that we understand the true nature of Islam, that we see it for what it really is. In fact, I will tell you this: I do not believe our country can truly fulfill its divine purpose until we understand our historical conflict with Islam. I know that this statement sounds extreme, but I do not shrink from its implications. The fact is that America was founded, in part, with the intention of seeing this false religion destroyed, and I believe September 11, 2001, was a generational call to arms that we can no longer ignore. (http://www.motherjones.com/washington_dispatch/2008/03/john-mccain-rod-parsley-spiritual-guide.html)

Parsley claims that Christopher Columbus sought to reach America in order to war with the Muslims and that Muslims are inherently violent. According to Parsley, "Allah was a demon spirit." That is why, it must be assumed, he's concerned that there are 1209 mosques in the United States. They're devil-worshippers. Indeed, Parsley called Islam an "anti-Christ religion."

John McCain sought and received Pastor Parsley's endorsement, and he praised Parsley for Parsley's "guidance" and "leadership." According to Corn, McCain went so far as to call Parsley a "spiritual guide." Parsley, then, was like Pastor Hagee, who "fairly often" provides McCain with "spiritual guidance."

Both pastors view America as having a biblical obligation, even a predestination, to lead its people in a war against Islam.

John McCain's ideas of religion, war, and religiously–inspired war mirror those of pastors Hagee and Parsley. As described in the previous chapter, McCain exhorts Americans to accept God's "providence" that our nation take on the role of the "New Jerusalem." It is our destined role in history, and presumably in the end-times too, to take on, as McCain puts it, our "sacred duty":

> We are part of something providential: a great experiment to prove to the world that democracy is not only the most effective form of government, but the only moral government. And through the years, generation after generation of Americans has held fast to the belief that we were meant to transform history. What greater cause than that could we ever find?

In McCain's world, it seems only logical that the "New Jerusalem" reserve the "Old Jerusalem" for the "chosen people" and no one else, as Hagee has called for. McCain parallels Hagee and Parsley in their views that the United States has a *predestined role in the history (and presumably the end times) of this world*. The United States is the font of morality for the world, and we must "impart our values upon humanity," as McCain has said.

We, the United States, will save the world, and even the Jewish people will accept Christ just as the U.S. commences a pre-emptive war with Iran, which brings on a cataclysmic clash with Islam, which will bring on the Armageddon. Of course, this paragraph combines the visions of all three of these American "prophets".

McCain's singular vision seems a bit more mundane. He does seem to believe that our "sacred duty" to impart our values upon humanity can be achieved through war, and McCain even seems to apply the Protestant "work ethic" *to military activities*. According McCain, too many Americans are lazy "hucksters" focused on our own "material" well-being and not focused on our "sacred duty" to the rest of the world. To this end, apparently, McCain voted *against* a revamped GI Bill designed to help U.S. soldiers pay for their college education. He worried that, rather than continue their work for the U.S. military, soldiers would quit the military to attend college. His vote jibes with his stated plans to expand the military, develop new branches of the military, and to keep the U.S. involved in various military conflicts.

Our work ethic will be tested. We may need to institute a draft. But all of this military stuff will have to pass through a skeptical Congress, right?

HOW WE WILL GO TO WAR

On CNBC's Republican debate, Chris Matthews asked John McCain if he would have to receive Congressional authorization for a strategic "attack on weaponry" in Iran. McCain answered, "I would at minimum *consult with the leaders of Congress* because there may come a time where you need the approval of Congress and I believe that this is a possibility that is maybe closer to reality than we are discussing tonight."

Two conclusions. First, *McCain would start a war against Iran without a Congressional "declaration of war," as the U.S. Constitution requires.* He would be willing to start a war with Iran with only a *consultation* with leaders of Congress. Which leaders? The Committee chairs? What happens if those committee chairs are Republicans? "Wow, that was easy; what other wars can I start?"

What happens when those Congressional leaders say "no"? McCain said that he would only *consult*, not seek *approval* of Congressional leaders. Although McCain prefers "strict constructionist" Supreme Court justices, his own beliefs about the powers of the president seem absolutely unconstitutional.

Second, McCain is trying to clue us in on what he plans on doing as President. Matthews was speaking of a "strategic attack" as if it were a very strong possibility. McCain wants the public to understand that he believes such an attack is even "closer to reality" than Matthews and the other Republican candidates believe.

If Bush and McCain continue to work together on issues of war, Bush could start a war with Iran even before McCain takes office. McCain would then be spared the hassle of convincing the American people to start another war. It is not that difficult to start a war. A glance at history tells us that if McCain were to launch an attack on suspected nuclear facilities in Iran and if Iran shot down one our planes, war would be only proper.

There are a million ways to start a war with a nation already labeled a "rogue state" or "Evil."

It is of course crass to put odds on the probability of war. But it is also important for voters to quantify the probability that a presidential candidate will launch our nation into wars. My instinct tells me that the odds are 95 to 5 that McCain will start a new war, whether that war is a small one (killing only thousands) or a large one (killing hundreds of thousands or millions). The number killed will depend on the circumstances. A successful small war, like our most recent war in Panama, may foster confidence in a larger war.

If McCain does launch our nation into war, I estimate 95 to 5 odds that one of the nations we will war with is Iran.

One way of deducing how many wars and against what nations a candidate might initiate war is by looking at the lobbyists and strategists that that candidate has hired to run his campaign. Like Karl Rove and Dick Cheney, campaign managers tend to turn themselves into cabinet members and high level executives in the new administration. Recall that Cheney was originally hired by Bush to help Bush search for a vice-presidential running mate, not to be vice-president.

But so many of the world's most abhorrent governments are represented by lobbyists at the highest levels of the McCain campaign that it is impossible to discern from this bloody tangle exactly which nation these lobbyists would most wish to start a war in. The United States often starts wars with precisely one of the repugnant dictators it has armed. In that case, McCain's lobbyists might prefer a war with one of the many dictatorships they have represented: Nigeria has a lot of oil, so that boosts their chances.

In the end, we will be at war, and we will ask how we got there. Perhaps we should ask that question first, before we elect John McCain.

RACE AND RACISM AT HOME

Bao Nguyen had it right. Just because someone apologizes does not mean that everything is okay.

Will McCain kick off a "civil rights rollback"?

Will John McCain attempt to repeal the 1964 Civil Rights Act or the 1965 Voting Rights Act? This would be impossible, politically. As evidenced by his votes against the Civil Rights Act of 1990 and the Equal Pay Act for women, McCain will likely cripple the enforcement of civil rights.

John McCain will likely continue the Bush Administration's policy of ignoring the Voting Rights Act. The suppression of black votes, of course, helped to get George W. Bush into the White House. Twice. The voting "irregularities" padded his votes in Florida in 2000 and in Ohio in 2004. And yet, little has been done to ensure that black voters, and voters in general, will be able to vote and have their votes counted. In fact, voting machines are now computerized and can be hacked into (tampered with) easily.

Fraud is now easier, but the desire to suppress black votes is just as great.

The general accuracy of the vote in America is shaky. And that benefits Republicans, as the right-wing party in America has always tended to benefit from "voting irregularities." Today, most of the Southern states, including Texas, South Carolina, Tennessee, Louisiana, Georgia, and Arkansas do not require voter verified paper records of each and every vote. Other states that do not require such paper verification are Kansas, Virginia, Kentucky, Pennsylvania, and Indiana. As a result, voters must trust that no one tampers with the computers on which the votes are stored. No recounts are possible.

Another eight states do not require paper copies of votes, but claim that voting stations are collecting paper records voluntarily.

In a McCain administration, voting rights will likely be a low priority. Why? African Americans tend to be the first group to be left out of the vote, intimidated out of voting, vote at stations that close early, get phone calls that tell them to vote on the wrong day, or get taken off voting rolls "accidentally." And African Americans will vote overwhelmingly against McCain. That's why.

Perhaps we can find hope in McCain's response to Hurricane Katrina, which has emerged as the major racial issue of our day. The treasonous federal response to Katrina cost the lives of hundreds or thousands of Americans, most of them black.

Republican senators and congressmen found it exceedingly difficult to come near Louisiana right after Hurricane Katrina. Instead, they spoke on Fox News Channel about how unfair it was that the rest of the nation should pay for a natural disaster in New Orleans. There is a famous photo of John McCain and George Bush celebrating McCain's birthday in the middle of the Katrina catastrophe, but can this really be held against McCain? One might say, "John McCain flew to Alabama to campaign in three cities for the white supremacist George Wallace, Jr., but he couldn't find Alabama or Louisiana on a map during Katrina."

But this may not be an accurate measure of McCain's resolve on this issue. What has McCain himself said?

After witnessing the devastation that federal apathy had wreaked, McCain still refused to commit to rebuilding the largely African American 9th Ward of New Orleans. When asked about it, McCain responded, "I really don't know. That's why I am going... We need to go back to have a conversation about what to do: rebuild it, tear it down, you know, whatever it is."

"Whatever it is" likely means buying out the low-income people of color who live in the 9th Ward or waiting until they abandon the devastated area and then allowing real estate developers to scoop up the properties at fire sale prices. The developers will then rebuild it as a neighborhood for wealthy people. It is hardly unprecedented, and it is the most logical explanation for McCain's reluctance to commit to rebuilding a neighborhood devastated by a hurricane *three years ago*.

Outside of the obvious issues of voting rights and the excruciatingly slow Katrina recovery, the broadest effects of a McCain administration on people of color in the U.S. may stem from the types of people that McCain appoints for executive office. John McCain has shown a penchant for paying hundreds of thousands of dollars to white supremacists/neo-Confederates. He has sought out the endorsements and work of racists, sexists, homophobes, and bloody lobbyists.

McCain has made no commitment that the people he will appoint to his cabinet will be any different from the people running his campaign. How might George Wallace, Jr. behave as the director of the Equal Employment Opportunity Commission? Might McCain appoint a segregationist like John Ashcroft to the Supreme Court? How about Terry Nelson as the Secretary of Education? Could John McCain stop himself from appointing white supremacist Richard Quinn as the director of the Civil Rights Commission?

OUR FUTURE

John McCain is a maverick. He does things that others would never do. And he does not care what other people think.

Out of the hundreds of thousands of Republicans running for office in 2006, John McCain endorsed a man who makes speeches for white supremacists.

Out of all the terrible names that McCain could have called his captors in Vietnam, he chose to use a racial epithet that demeans all Asians and Asian Americans.

Out of all the jokes John McCain could crack about the Clinton family, he chose a mean-spirited, sexist, homophobic attack on Chelsea Clinton.

Out of all the Republican strategists available in the American South, John McCain chose a white supremacist.

Out of all the issues McCain could have taken a stand on, he decided to raise the Confederate battle flag in the middle of a divisive debate over that flag.

Out of all the presidents that McCain could have chosen to emulate, McCain chose a racist warmonger.

Out of all the federal policies John McCain could have protested — military aid to dictators, pork barrel boondoggles — John McCain decided that the Martin Luther King holiday had simply taken things too far.

Do I think John McCain is a racist? Yes, I call him a racist.

Whatever.

What is truly of concern is that he is a powerful, active, war–loving racist.

That matters. It matters not only to people of color in the United States. It matters to all Americans.

And not only does it matter to Americans.

The future of people worldwide is at stake.

Those people, the people of the world, we the people, are people. People. No more, and certainly no less. They, we, all of us and each of us, are not gooks, and we the people will work towards a future where not a single person is thought of, or called, a gook.

The first day of that future may or may not be January 20, 2009.

Herbert J. Seligman, "The Conquest of Haiti," *The Nation*, July 10, 1920

from Selections from The Nation magazine, 1865–1990, edited by Katerina Vanden Heuvel, Thunder's Mouth Press, 1990, paper, available at *http://www.thirdworldtraveler.com/Independent_Media/Conquest_Haiti_SNM.html*

Paul A. Kramer, *The Blood of Government: Race, Empire, the United States, and the Philippines*, UNC Press, 2006.

Zinn, Howard, *A People's History of the United States: 1492–Present*, Perennial Classics, 2003.

Nebrida, Victor, "The Balangiga Massacre: Getting Even," available at *http://www.bibingka.com/phg/balangiga/default.htm*

Welch, Richard E., "American Atrocities in the Philippines: The Indictment and the Response," *The Pacific Historical Review*, Vol. 43, No. 2 (May, 1974), pp. 233–253

Thomas, Emil, letters, 1923 to 1929, available from Ohio University, *https://www.library.ohiou.edu/archives/mss/mss192.pdf*

Korean War veterans posts at *http://www.koreanwar.org/html/units/usmc/7mareg_at.htm*

Jules Archer quote in *The Plot to Seize the White House*, out of print. Available at *http://www.clubhousewreckards.com/plot/plottoseizethewhitehouse.htm*

Metzger, Thomas, DESTROY ALL GOO–GOOS (America's Forgotten War), 1999, *http://www.loompanics.com/Articles/DestroyAllGooGoos.htm*

Roediger, David, "Gook: The short history of an Americanism," in *Towards the Abolition of Whiteness: Essays on Race, Politics, and Working-Class History* (London: Verso, 1994).

Powers, Thomas, "Oh, What an Ugly War," *New York Times Magazine*, Jan. 10, 1999.

On war crimes hearings, see *http://members.aol.com/warlibrary/vwch7.htm*

McCain, John, HOW THE POW's FOUGHT BACK, *US News & World Report*, May 14, 1973.

McCain, John, "Barry Goldwater, Patriot and Politician", *Washington Post*, 5/30/1998

McCain, John, *Faith of My Fathers*, Random House, 1999.

"DNC: John McCain's Real Record on MLK Holiday," 4 April 2008, Targeted News

Service.

"McCain's Tribute To MLK Spotlights His Opposition To MLK Day, Support Of Confederate Flag," see http://thinkprogress.org/2008/04/04/mccain-mlk/

Stein, Sam, "McCain won't apologize for vote against Civil Rights Bill," see http://www.huffingtonpost.com/2008/04/11/mccains-other-controversi_n_96193.html

Regarding McCain and Alabama whites only club: http://www.rawstory.com/news/2007/Sen._McCain_once_against_King_holiday_0115.html

Simon, Roger, Divided We Stand: How Al Gore Beat George Bush and Lost the Presidency, Crown, 2001.

Simon, Roger, U.S. News & World Report, Sept. 27, 1999.

Brock, David and Paul Waldman, Free Ride: John McCain and the Media, Anchor Books, 2008.

"Profile: American Maverick," Sunday Business Post, 25 February 2007.

Dreyfuss, Robert, "McCain's Vietnam," The Nation, Jan. 3, 2000.

Thomma Stevenand and Ben Stocking, "MCCAIN IS DEFIANT ABOUT HIS USE OF ANTI-ASIAN TERM," Knight-Ridder News Service, 18 February 2000

"Racial Issues Dog GOP Foes," Terry M. Neal; Edward Walsh , Washington Post, Feb. 18, 2000.

Nevius, C.W., Marc Sandalow, John Wildermuth, "McCain Criticized for Slur," San Francisco Chronicle, Feb. 18, 2000.

CLAY ROBISON, R.G. RATCLIFFE, CRAGG HINES, "Campaign 2000/ McCain defends use of ethnic slur to describe captors," Houston Chronicle, 18 February 2000

Houston Chronicle/Viewpoints, 24 February 2000

THOMMA, Steven, Ben Stocking, "McCain's racial slur upsets Asians POLITICS: But a Westminster attorney says South Vietnamese understand the context: against his captors." Knight Ridder Newspapers, 18 February 2000.

Tilove, Johnathon, "MCCAIN'S RACIAL SLUR IS ECHOING IN NEAR-SILENCE," Newhouse News Service, 4 March 2000, The Oregonian.

Thomas D. Elias, Thomas D., "McCain epithet angers U.S. Asians; Vietnam refugees in California not unsympathetic," THE WASHINGTON TIMES, February 25, 2000.

Howard Kurtz, Howard, "Up Again, McCain Taps The Messengers; The Candidate Makes Use Of Local Media on His Trail," *Washington Post*, Feb. 24, 2000.

"Chalk up McCain's slur to "human nature", says US official in Hanoi," *Deutsche Presse-Agentur*, Feb. 22, 2000

Watkin, Huw, "War hero's saviour wants 'gook' apology," *The Australian*, Feb. 24, 2000.

"No Place for Epithets," letter to editor, *The New York Times*, Feb. 25, 2000.

Moxley, R. Scott and Vu Nguyen, "Quiet Riot," *Orange County Weekly*, March 9, 2000, see *http://www.ocweekly.com/news/news/quiet-riot/23620/*

Rene Sanchez, "In Little Saigon, the Past Greets John McCain," *Washington Post*, Mar 3, 2000.

"Bush is confident S.C. 'fire wall' can contain McCain," *St. Petersburg Times*, Florida, Feb 19, 2000.

"Media Advisory: Southern Partisan: Setting the Record Straight," Fairness and Accuracy In Reporting, *http://www.fair.org/index.php?page=1880*

Parker, Suzi and Jake Tapper, "McCain's ancestors owned slaves," Feb. 15, 2000, Salon.com, *http://www.salon.com/politics2000/feature/2000/02/15/mccain*

"RICHARD QUINN & ASSOCIATES," January 2, 2008, *http:// politicalconsultantmisconduct.blogspot.com/2008/01/richard-quinn-associates-employee-of.html*

Yardley, Jonathon, "A Banner Year for Racists," *Washington Post*, Jan. 17, 2000.

St. Petersburg Times (Florida), "McCain flag apology extraordinary," editorial, April 21, 2000. See also *St. Petersburg Times* (Florida) papers, of January and February, 2000.

Lester, Will, "Who voted in South Carolina and why," Associated Press, Feb. 19, 2000

People for the American Way on Richard Quinn and Southern Partisan, *http://www.pfaw.org/pfaw/general/default.aspx?oid=2581*

Prince, K. Michael, *Rally 'round the Flag, Boys!: South Carolina and the Confederate Flag*, University of South Carolina Press, 2004.

Holmes, Steven, "After Campaigning on Candor, McCain Admits He Lacked It on Confederate Flag Issue," *The New York Times*, April 20, 2000.

CNN, Larry King Live, South Carolina Republican Debate, Aired February 15, 2000 - 9:00 p.m. ET, see *http://transcripts.cnn.com/TRANSCRIPTS/0002/15/lkl.00.html*

On McCain visit to contra camp, see Washington Post, Feb. 9, 1988; also, September 2, 1987, *Washington Post*.

On Witness for Peace: *http://www.doublestandards.org/wakeup1.html*

"McCain Camp touts Ollie North Endorsement," Juliet Eilperin and Rena Kirsch, *Washington Post*, Feb. 12, 2008, see *http://blog.washingtonpost.com/the-trail/2008/02/12/mccain_camp_touts_ollie_north.html*

'I PROMISED TO TELL THE TRUTH ALWAYS ... I FELL SHORT,' MCCAIN SAYS, *The Boston Globe*, April 20, 2000.

Hulse, Carl, "Senate Passes a Bill That Favors English." *The New York Times*, May 19, 2006.

Hurt, Charles, "Reid calls language proposal racist," *The Washington Times*, May 31, 2006.

Southern Poverty Law Center, "Sharks in the Mainstream: Racism underlies influential 'conservative' group," *Intelligence Report*, Winter 1999; see *http://www.splcenter.org/intel/intelreport/article.jsp?aid=360*

Southern Poverty Law Center, "Counsel of Citizens: Coffee, beer and white supremacy," *http://www.splcenter.org/intel/intelreport/article.jsp?sid=237*

Carter, Dan, T., *The Politics of Rage: George Wallace, the Origins of the New Conservatism and the Transformation of American Politics*, LSU Press, 2000.

Leshar, Stephen, *George Wallace: American Populist*, Da Capo Press, 1995.

"McCain campaigns for George Wallace Jr.," 21 November 2005, AP Newswires.

"McCain to visit Alabama to endorse Wallace," 17 November 2005, AP Newswires.

"McCain and George Wallace, Jr.," National Journal, Nov. 18, 2005, see *http://hotlineblog.nationaljournal.com/archives/2005/11/mccain_and_geor.html*

The Council of Conservative Citizens website: *www.cofcc.org* (recently got warning that accessing this website may be harmful to my computer).

"Who is McCain campaign manager Terry Nelson? And will the media tell us?" Media Matters fro America, Dec. 13, 2006, *http://mediamatters.org/items/200612130001*

"Terry Nelson," Sourcewatch, *http://www.sourcewatch.org/index.php?title=Terry_Nelson*

"Crosslink Strategy Group: About us," *http://www.crosslinkstrategy.com/crosslink_contents/about/nelson.shtml*

"Scott Howell," Sourcewatch, *http://www.sourcewatch.org/index.php?title=Scott_Howell*

Moyers, Bill, "Bill Moyers Journal: Christians United For Israel," October 7, 2007, *http://www.pbs.org/moyers/journal/10052007/profile.html*

For McCain speech at Hagee conference, see Bill Moyers Journal: Christians United for Israel at *http://www.pbs.org/moyers/journal/03072008/profile.html*

For McCain interview with George Stephanopoulos, *This week with George Stephanopoulos*, ABC News.

Berkowitz, Bill, "Defending Israel to the 'End Times'" Jan. 29, 2008, *http://www.mediatransparency.org/story.php?storyID=226*

"McCain courts apocalypse pastor, Hagee," *http://www.alternet.org/blogs/peek/48397/*

Wilson, Bruce, "McCain-backer Hagee's 'Thrilling' Worldview: Rapture, Then "Holocaust" Feb. 29, 2008, *http://www.talk2action.org/story/2008/2/29/115039/049*

Corn, David, "McCain's Spiritual Guide: Destroy Islam," *Mother Jones*, March 12, 2008, *http://www.motherjones.com/washington_dispatch/2008/03/john-mccain-rod-parsley-spiritual-guide.html*

Schecter, Cliff, *The Real McCain: Why Conservatives Don't Trust Him and Why Independents Shouldn't*, Polipoint Press, 2008.

Lobe, Jim, "Policy Report: 'Committee for the Liberation of Iraq' sets up shop," *Foreign Policy in Focus*, Nov. 2002.

The Iraqi National Congress website: *http://www.inciraq.com/*

Drogin, Bob, "John McCain is betting big on Iraq: His long-sought 'surge' is working now, but he's been wrong too." *LA Times*, March 23, 2008, see *http://www.latimes.com/news/nationworld/nation/la-na-mccainiraq23mar23,1,5646789.story*

For a very disturbing look at the lobbyists working for McCain see "McCain's Lobbyists In Trouble For Foreign Lobbying" Progressive Media USA, May 11, 2008; available at *http://www.mccainsource.com/mccain_fact_check?id=0007*

"The Pentagon Muzzles the CIA," Dreyfuss, Richard, *The American Prospect*, Dec. 16, 2002.

Welch, Matt, *McCain: Myth of a Maverick*, Macmillan, 2008.

For McCain's USC speech, "ADDRESS BY SENATOR JOHN MCCAIN UNIVERSITY OF SOUTHERN CALIFORNIA IDES OF MARCH DINNER," March 25, 2002, available at official John McCain website; see *http://mccain.senate.gov/public/index.*

cfm?FuseAction=PressOffice.Speeches&ContentRecord_id=2527d207-45c5-4b46-9d68-abceobf4416b&Region_id=&Issue_id=

On McCain speech saying that there will be 'more wars' see *http://rawstory.com/news/2007/McCain_straight_talk_Expect_more_war_0127.html*

Charlie Rose Show, PBS, May 15, 2008.

Hammer, David, "McCain: Response to Katrina 'terrible'" by David Hammer, *The New Orleans Times-Picayune*, Friday April 25, 2008; see *http://www.nola.com/news/index.ssf/2008/04/mccain_response_to_katrina_ter.html*.

Printed in the United States
115403LV00001B/127-225/P